TRUE FRIENDS

Life with Five Seeing Eye Dogs

Bill Meinecke

authorHOUSE®

AuthorHouse™
1663 Liberty Drive
Bloomington, IN 47403
www.authorhouse.com
Phone: 1-800-839-8640

First published by AuthorHouse   8/18/2009

ISBN: 978-1-4389-8050-8 (sc)
ISBN: 978-1-4389-8051-5 (hc)

Printed in the United States of America
Bloomington, Indiana

This book is printed on acid-free paper.

About the author

I was born in Flushing, New York, and was educated in a school for blind children. Then I mainstreamed into the public school system, where I graduated from high school. I have been using Seeing Eye dogs for forty years. I hold two master's degrees and live in Virginia Beach, Virginia, with my fifth dog, Nan.

Foreword

I have wanted to write this book for a long time. I made many attempts, but they have not borne fruit. Now I believe that it is time to write this long-awaited memoir. It is about my life with five Seeing Eye dogs. I will start about forty years ago when I got my first dog. I have had many good experiences with these dogs, and they have made my life very interesting. Not only were the dogs that I have had very good guides, but they were special companions and were unique. All of them have a special place in my heart. I hope that the reader will enjoy the experiences I had as much as I did. Having these dogs gave me the courage to do things that I probably would not have done otherwise, like going away to college; more on this later. I hope that the reader will realize the tremendous advantage one has in owning these dogs. They really enriched my life. It is amazing how I went from being shy and scared of traveling to visiting thirty-five states and flying close to three hundred thousand air miles in forty years. It all started with my first dog, and now I am working with my fifth dog, who is a lot of fun; more about her later. These dogs can be a tremendous asset for those who can and choose to use them. They are always ready to do their work no matter the time of day or night. I am glad I can share my experiences using these dogs. I hope that parents will read this book to their children, grandparents will read it to their grandchildren, and children will read and enjoy it. I am glad I am able to share my experiences with the reader.

A Seeing Eye dog takes about five to six months to be trained. They are born on the school's breeding farm, and then they live with puppy-raiser families until they are about eighteen months of age. They then come back to the school and train with a trainer for about four months. Their future owners, such as myself, then go to the school and train with the dog. We get to know them and they get to know us. After that they live and work with us for the rest of their lives.

Dedication

This book is dedicated to the five dogs that I have used during the past forty years and am still using. I would also like to dedicate this book to the staff of the Seeing Eye. Without their instruction and dedication to their mission, I would not be where I am today.

Acknowledgments

I would like to express my appreciation to Jean Brennan for her assistance with the artwork in this book. I would also like to thank Florence and John Gaffrey and Mary May for their help in getting materials together for the book.

Chapter 1 Sandra the pioneer

Training with Sandra

I had wanted to get a Seeing Eye dog for a long time. It was a dream I had always had since I was about eight years old when one of my teachers had a dog in the grade school that I attended. I was amazed that she could cross the street by herself. Being blind, I always wanted to be able to cross the street myself. The street in front of the house where I lived until I was about eleven years old was very busy, so my parents would not let me cross by myself. When I was eleven, we moved to a bigger house in the country, which presented a different challenge—no sidewalks. I learned to deal with this situation. I took cane travel when I was about fifteen and found that as good as it was, it wasn't as safe as I would have liked. I had a refresher course when I graduated from high school where they had us ride the New York subways. This made me nervous, because I felt that there was too much danger in that situation.

It was in 1968 that I decided to get the dog. I had a friend who had one, and he told me how good it was getting around with it. I had a couple of choices of schools, but in the spring of 1967, Walt Disney aired a show called "Atta Girl Kelly" about the Seeing Eye and how they trained their dogs. They took you through the whole process from bringing up the puppies and how kids in the area gave the pups a loving home and taught them skills that the dogs needed until they were old enough for training. They then showed you how the dogs were trained and how the blind student was trained with the dog. That convinced me that the Seeing Eye was the place to go. On March 12, 1969, when I was 20 years old I filled out the application for the Seeing Eye. I heard from them in a week. They told me that they were considering my application and were writing to the references that I provided. It was now time to wait and wonder if I would be accepted. I had to have a medical exam for the school. They wanted to make sure that I was healthy. I had the exam and everything was okay. We sent them the medical forms and waited. I waited until May 3, when I got a letter from them saying that I was accepted. I was relieved and excited at the same time. I was also a little scared. I hoped I would do well, but I was concerned that I would work with the dog and be able to trust her; more about that later.

July 8, 1969

In four days I would go to the Seeing Eye. I was getting excited and anxious at the same time. It would be a big change in my life, but a good one.

In 1969 the Vietnam War was raging and students were demonstrating against it. Two men were getting ready to walk on the moon; more about that later. The New York Mets were getting ready to win their first World Series. In fact, Tom Seaver almost pitched a perfect game. Woodstock, the biggest outdoor weekend gathering, was about to occur. On this day I started packing for Morristown, and this brought the occasion a lot closer. My parents, grandparents, brother, and I were going to drive to the Seeing Eye on Saturday, July 12. Four more days. I was sitting in my house, thinking that when I came home I would have a dog. What would the dog be like? Would I like it? Was I doing the right thing? I thought so. I had spent the past couple of months walking around the neighborhood as they suggested. This would give me the exercise that I needed to prepare for the dog, and it also helped me learn about the area. When you work a dog you have to know where you are going so you can do your share of the work. I was ready for whatever they dished out.

July 11

The day before we left I was really getting excited. I was going to be meeting a lot of new people: staff, students, and instructors.

What would it be like? We finished packing and planned for the drive to Morristown. The Seeing Eye thought of everything. They sent us detailed directions on how to get there from Long Island, where we lived. I was impressed with that.

July 12, 1969

This was the day I had been waiting for. I woke up about four that morning. We were having a thunderstorm, and I had to close the windows in my room. The storm did not last long, and I went back to sleep. I remember hearing the birds starting to sing at about 5:30. I was excited. We were going to the Seeing Eye that day, and the following day I would get the dog. Back in those days they gave us the dog the very next day after we got there. I was told this by my friend who had gotten a dog a couple of years earlier.

I got up and ate breakfast and we started loading up the car. The day was quite humid, and it looked like more rain. We had a 1966 Oldsmobile station wagon. It had three seats, so it gave us lots of room for the trip. My grandparents were going with us, so we needed room for six people. We drove from Huntington, Long Island, to Bayside, Queens, to pick up my grandparents. After having coffee at my grandparents' house we started out for Morristown.

As we came across the George Washington Bridge my brother said that it looked dark over New Jersey. That is interesting, I thought. As we drove along I heard big rain drops hitting the windshield of the car. We drove for an hour and it really started raining. When we started to approach Morristown the rain was coming down heavily. There were parts of the town where the streets were flooded and we had to detour. We finally got on the road that went to the Seeing Eye and started going out in the country. We were really getting close now, and I was both excited and anxious. We pulled onto the grounds, but we were not sure that it was the right place. The grounds looked very nice. It looked like a country club or something. Because it was raining, my father went in to make sure we were in the right place. When my father came out one of the instructors came with him carrying an umbrella. We got out of the car, and the gentlemen said, "Mr. Meinecke, I am your instructor." I didn't answer him at first because I didn't realize he was talking to me. We walked into the building, which was like a mansion. The place was beautiful. It had nice carpeting and was very fancy. I met Miss Paula Pursley, who coordinated the classes. She seemed very proper, as did all of the staff that I met. As the instructor showed me to my room, my parents, grandparents, and brother went on a tour of the building.

When I got to the room I noticed that it was very clean and spacious. Each room had a bathroom, like a hotel, and was air conditioned.

After about twenty minutes or so my parents and grandparents came back and told me that the building was beautiful. They showed them the lounges and the dining room. My brother told me that they were serving hamburgers for lunch and that I was lucky. We asked Mr. Areanas, the instructor, if I had a roommate, and he told me that I did—a gentleman from Florida. I thought that would be interesting.

My family then took me on a tour of the building. I saw the lounges and the dining room, which were very nice. My dad told me that we were on a hill overlooking a valley. The view was spectacular. We could see this view from the dining room. The dining room was fancy. I hoped that the food was going to be good. They took me to the main lounge, where my brother showed me the carrels that they had for a talking book, a Braille writer, and a typewriter. This sure was a beautiful place. We next went to Ms. Pursley's office to give her 150 dollars, which is what one pays for the first Seeing Eye dog. It is a token fee to show the public that we are willing to pay for something that means a lot to us. It is a way for us to gain self-respect. It was then time for my family to leave, and I felt anxious about that. I could not believe that I was actually there, but I wondered how things would go. Would I like this experience?

When they left I became very emotional. The experience was starting to get to me. I went back to my room to wait for them to call us down for lunch. It was then that I met Mr. Jim Gordon, who was another student from Binghamton, New York. He was there for his second dog. That was interesting.

We were then called down for lunch. It was in the dining room that I met Dan Booke and Doug Roberts. Mr. Booke was the head instructor, and Mr. Roberts was an apprentice. Today, Doug Roberts is head of all programs at the school—talk about moving up! We had those hamburgers and they were good. We were waited on like in a fancy restaurant.

After lunch we hung around the lounge and got acquainted. The instructor took me on a "Juno walk." This is when he pretends to be the dog. He is measuring your walking speed and how much of a pull you can tolerate. This is so they can match you up with the best dog for you. We walked around the campus; it was quite humid. The rain stopped for a while. He told me that I did very well. He mentioned that we would get the dog the following day. I was excited about that.

During the afternoon, the rest of the class began to arrive. They came from Florida, Massachusetts, Idaho, New York, Tennessee, and Missouri. That was quite a cross-section of the United States. My roommate arrived, and we got acquainted before dinner.

Dinner was another great meal in the fancy dining room. The class was all there, and Mr. Areanas introduced us all and mentioned where we came from. We all enjoyed the meal, which was elaborately served by waitresses.

After dinner we went with the instructor into the Eustis Lounge, named after the founder of the school, Dorothy Harrison Eustis. This lounge was nicely furnished and had carpeting in it. It was like someone's fancy living room. He talked to us about what to expect in the class. He went over what would happen tomorrow when we would receive the dogs. This made me excited. We then had a chance to ask questions, and after that he took us on a formal tour of the building. We found out where all of the offices were and where the laundry was. It was all very nice and clean. We were then given our leashes, which we would use the next day. This was great. We were also given the grooming equipment. This brought the dog a lot closer.

For the rest of the evening we just hung out and got acquainted with each other. This was good, because the next day was going to be very busy.

July 13

The next morning when I woke up I heard dogs barking in the kennels on the campus. I wondered which dog out there was mine. I looked at the bed chain that was attached to the wall next to my bed and thought, *Tonight there will be a dog attached to it.*

During breakfast we met Mr. Debetas, who was the head of training. He had been there since the school was founded. I was impressed with that. After breakfast all of the groups had a lecture with Mr. Myrose, who gave us the house rules and told us what to expect in the class. We then went on another Juno walk in town. The instructor acted like the dog, just as the day before, but this time we were on the sidewalks of Morristown. This was exciting. After we got back from the walk, Jay Hill, one of the students, entertained us by playing the piano. He was really good at it. All three instructors disappeared. We found out that they were having the final meeting to determine which dogs we would get.

Just before lunch Mr. Areanas came back and got us together to tell us which dogs we would get. We all held our breath as we were given the news. I found out that I would have a collie and German shepherd mix named Sandra. My roommate was getting a German shepherd named Vera. We were all excited, talking about the dogs we were going to get. This would happen after lunch.

The lunch was a very nice meal, and for dessert one of the students had a birthday, so we had cake and ice cream. The school had a policy that on your birthday they would give you a cake. I would celebrate my birthday during the class.

After lunch we were told to go back to our rooms and wait for our dogs. I was excited and scared at the same time. Would Sandra like me? We would soon see. It was about two in the afternoon of Sunday July 13, 1969, a day I would never forget. A big change in my life was about to occur. I lay on my bed, waiting for things to happen. I asked my roommate how he was doing, and he said that he was excited. I told him how I felt, and he said that he could understand. The big moment was at hand. I heard movement in the room next door. I could hear a dog whimpering in the room that Jim and Jay were in. They probably had their dogs. It would soon be our turn. The instructor knocked at the door and asked my roommate to come with him. He went somewhere and was gone a few minutes. He then came back with his dog. The dog was panting and whimpering. He petted and talked to the dog. I asked if she was nice, and he said she was.

Then I heard a chain being used in the next room. The instructor came and asked me to come with him with the dog's leash that we had received the night before. I was really nervous. The big moment had arrived. We went into a room and he closed the door. I heard a dog panting. He told me to call Sandra, and he gave me a ball of ground meat to give her. I called her, and she came over and took the meat. I stroked her soft coat. She was wonderful. I put the leash on her and patted her. Mr. Areanas asked me if I liked her, and I told him that I liked her very much. I saw that her ears were pointed straight up. She was very quiet and wanted to be with the instructor. He told me that in time she would bond with me. I took her back to my room and sat on my bed. She was whimpering and panting. She looked at the door like she did not want to be with me. When I told her that she was a good girl, she wagged her tail. I petted her and told her that we would get to know each other. She did not want any part of me, and I was disappointed. I found that I would have to win her over. This would take time.

After about an hour the instructor came back; Sandra wagged her tail when she saw him. He asked how we were doing, and I said okay. When he left, she whimpered like she missed him. She probably did. I was thinking, *Gosh I hope she gets to like me.*

About four the instructor came back and took the dogs out to the park. We would go out there later that evening. It was raining hard, so the dogs were wet when they came back in. When he brought Sandra, she wagged her tail when she saw me.

We then brought the dogs to the dining room for supper. We were taught how to put the dogs down under the table. They behaved very well. While we were eating, they just stayed under the table at our feet. I was impressed with that.

After supper we hung around the lounge until eight o'clock; then we took the dogs out to the park. This was a paved area behind the building where the dogs took care of their biological needs. They showed us what the dogs were doing. I was amazed with that. Gosh, they thought of everything. I was wondering how we would know what the dogs were doing. All we had to do was feel their back. After the dogs were finished, we hung around the lounge until about ten, and then I went to bed. We would have a big day the next day. Sandra lay down on the carpet that they gave us and went to sleep.

July 14

The next morning we woke up around 5:45, which was early. The instructor knocked on the door and told us that it was time to get up. He gave us food for the dogs. Sandra really enjoyed hers. We then took them outside like the evening before. Sandra took care of herself nicely. It was daylight and cool. We then got ready for the day. After breakfast, which was very good, we took our first trip into Morristown. When we were on the sidewalk I was very excited. The harness was on her and we were ready to go. We started when I said, "Forward." She moved out nicely. The instructor had a leash around my wrist. After about a block he took the leash off and I was free; it felt wonderful. We did a short route on residential streets. We passed one area that had a big crack in the sidewalk caused by a big tree. This taught us to follow the dog. We also had to cross a couple of streets that were residential. Sandra did great. I got back to the van feeling great. I gave her a big hug and told her that she was a good girl.

That afternoon we did the same route. It was hot, and she started to pant while we were out on the street. She did well again.

The next day we did the same route, and she did well going around a tree right in the middle of the sidewalk. That impressed me. We did the same walk that afternoon in the hot weather. On Wednesday, I was waiting in the van after my walk, and my friend had a radio and I was able to listen as three men blasted off for the moon. That was quite a time in our nation's history. We did the same route in the morning and the afternoon.

On Thursday we did the route for our first solo. It was very hot, and we had to walk up one block and make a left, go one block and make a left on a busy street, and walk three blocks and make another left. We then walked one block and made another left and walked two blocks and made a right back to the van. Sandra did this very well. I was sweating after that trip, but it was good walking at a fast pace. We did this route on Friday and had our first solo on Saturday morning.

On Saturday afternoon I had guests. We could have guests on Saturday and Sunday afternoons between two and four PM. It was nice having family come out and see the school. They took pictures of me and Sandra, and that was good.

That evening we had pizza and other things and the instructors told stories about their experiences with training dogs. We all had a good time and were able to relax after the week.

Sunday, July 20

The next morning I went to church, but we had to leave the dogs at the school. When I got back Sandra was very quiet and didn't seem to want anything to do with me. After lunch I sat on the floor in my room and talked with her and patted her and told her that she was a good girl. She seemed better after that. I had more company that afternoon; a former teacher came to visit me, and that was a surprise.

Later we watched two men land on the moon. I was sitting next to Jackie Graham, who was a very pretty girl in my group. I was glad I was sitting next to her. It was awesome watching those men land on the moon. That evening after we took the dogs out, the two men walked on the moon's surface. That was quite a landmark in our nation's history. We watched all of it.

July 21

The next day we started our second week. We were preparing for another solo. This one was more complicated. We went one block and then made a left and walked five blocks. We made a couple of curves, and the area was busy with traffic and people walking through the center of town. After the five blocks we made a left on South Street and went two blocks near the square. We made another left and went to the van. The route took about twenty-five minutes, give or take. We would solo Wednesday morning. Sandra seemed to know the route and did it very well. We practiced it in the morning and the afternoon. It was drizzling, but that was okay. After the afternoon trip I relaxed, and that evening we learned obedience exercises. This is where we have the dog come and sit at our side and we have them fetch things like sticks and gloves. Sandra liked doing that. I gave her a hug when she did it well.

We had two practice trips on Tuesday, and things went well.

On Wednesday, the day of the solo, I had to take Sandra out a couple of times during the night. She had diarrhea. In fact, most of the dogs had it. To make things worse, it was raining when we took them out. Consequently, I didn't get much sleep that night. We had to do the solo and it was raining. They told us that we would work the dogs in all types of weather, and they were right.

The solo did not go as great as I would have wanted it to go. My partner did not get around very well, and she kept thinking that we were lost. We would travel in pairs and we would help each other out. She could not help me out, and I had to do everything myself. Besides, it was pouring and I was tired from the night before. Somehow we got through the trip, and I was glad to get back in that van where it was dry.

That afternoon we did not go out. It was raining too hard. We had a meeting about the trip that morning, and I was able to relax and take a nap after the night before.

That evening we watched the Seeing Eye's public relations film. They have films to educate the public about the program. We went to bed and slept much better and got ready for the next day.

On Thursday morning we went to the railroad station, which I was interested in because I would be riding the Long Island Railroad a lot. Sandra did well there. After we were finished we waited in the downtown lounge that the school has. The instructor told me that the dog would take me into the lounge. I wondered how she would do that, but she did, and I thought that was cool. In the afternoon we started going over the high school route, the longest route that we would solo on. We would have the solo for that on Saturday, and it would take about forty-five minutes to walk that route. We worked on that Thursday afternoon, Friday morning, and Friday afternoon. We had the solo on Saturday morning, and it went well. Needless to say, my feet were tired after that solo. We walked on streets that went uphill or down, so we got our exercise.

We had the rest of the day off, which was good. That night we had pizza again, and we were very glad to relax with the dogs and our fellow students. On Sunday we had a big dinner, and my parents came out to visit me. They were impressed with Sandra, and I told them that they would get to know her. I discovered that Sandra did not like cats. They have a cat roaming around the grounds to see how the dogs react to such a distraction. Well, Sandra did not like that cat. I was able to control her, and my parents and I had a good visit.

That evening we had a cookout for supper. That cat came by again, and I had to hold Sandra down because she was shivering with fury. If she could have gotten loose, that cat would have been history. We all enjoyed the cookout; it was a hot day.

On Monday, July 28, we started what they called freelancing. It was also my birthday. I didn't tell anyone about it, but some of the staff knew about it so they wished me a happy birthday. We were having heavy showers that morning, and we walked around town and went into a building with an elevator. For some reason Sandra did not like that elevator. She really wanted to get out of it. I was concerned about that, but the instructor said that it was because the elevator was small. When we were walking we had to go on a porch because it was raining so hard.

That afternoon we went to Woolworth's and had a Coke and went to Bamberger's store and rode another elevator. The instructor told us to follow our dogs when we got out on this particular floor. We walked around the floor and followed the dogs. They did great. When we got back in the elevator, the instructor told us that we were in the China Department. There were racks of very expensive china on each side of us. One wrong turn and it would have been very expensive if we shattered all of that china. That experience really showed me how great these dogs were. Had I known we were going to the China Department, I don't know if I would have been so eager. Sandra came through, though.

That night at supper they gave me a birthday cake. I was touched by that. Here they were remembering my birthday. That was great. We hung around the lounge for the rest of the evening. My parents called me to wish me a happy birthday.

For the rest of the week we did more freelancing. We went into more stores, took the dogs into coffee shops, and walked in different areas of Morristown.

On Thursday the retrains—the students who had been there before—went home. I was sad to see them go. On Friday we took a bus trip. Sandra went under the seat and was very good. That afternoon we walked to the school from town. It consisted of country roads, walking through a park, and walking in the woods. You heard about New Jersey mosquitoes; well, they were out there. We were eaten alive.

We had our last weekend at the school. We hung around and went swimming on Saturday. We had another cookout on Sunday. We were getting ready to have our last couple of days.

On Monday, August 4, we started our last week. We would go home on Thursday. It was raining, and we walked around Morristown and went to a coffee shop to give the dogs that experience. In the afternoon we walked around town and went to a department store where we walked with the dogs in the narrow aisles of the store. This taught us to follow our dogs. That evening the students who were flying home were told when their flights were. I felt bad that I was not flying home. I thought it would be cool to be flying home. Little did I know that I would someday be flying more than all of my classmates combined!

On Tuesday afternoon we took the train to Dover, New Jersey. This would be good because Sandra and I would be taking the Long Island Railroad a lot. She did very well. On Wednesday we just walked around town to finish up. I was proud of how well she did in the class.

Thursday, August 7, was a warm summer day, and we were all going home with our dogs. My parents did not get there until around noon, so I was the last to leave. We had air conditioning in the car, so we would be cool on the drive home. On the way home Sandra got sick, so we had to stop and let her out to take care of Sandra's needs. I was nervous about that. We stopped in at my grandparents' house, and she took me right into the house very well. That was great, even though she had not been there before. Then we went home and I relaxed and showed her around the house as we were instructed to do.

A new life

So now I was home with Sandra. That evening I spent time having my family come into the living room of the house to meet her. We had to do this so that every person in my family would get a chance to get acquainted with her. I wanted to keep her as close to the routine of the school as possible when I first got home, so that evening I took her out to groom her. She felt comfortable with that. When I was at the school I wondered if she really liked me. She would always get excited when the instructor would enter the room. I learned that night that I had finally won her over. She would growl at everyone who would come into my room. She somehow came to the realization that I was her master. She thought that she had to protect me.

The next day I woke up about six and took her outside. She was okay, but you could tell that she felt a little strange. After breakfast we took a short walk in the neighborhood. I was really nervous. I wondered if I had learned enough. I wondered what would happen if she acted up. What would I do? We took our walk and she did great. She remembered where my house was, which I thought was fantastic.

I learned over the first month we were together that these dogs have their personalities. Sandra was very protective of me around other dogs. She would go nuts when she saw another dog come near me. Also, she did not like being petted very much. I would pet her, but she would then go away and lie down in her favorite spots in the house. We had a stairway that had a landing on it, and she loved to lie on the landing and look out the front door, which was right next to it. She could see what was going on.

During the first year we were together, I took it easy. I was deciding what college I was going to go to. During that time I took my first trip by train into New York to look at a possible school I would attend.

Sandra was great on the train, lying under the seat. I took another trip into New York with a friend who had a dog from another school. People remarked how well Sandra did going through the subways and things. She really handled the city traffic very well.

It was during that time that I took my first trip by air; one of many that I would take with her. She lay at my feet and was very good during the takeoff and landing. She almost enjoyed it. It was that next summer that I decided to go to junior college. We went out and signed up for classes. So now Sandra was going to be a college girl.

Junior college

In September of 1970 I started college. Sandra and I had to learn the campus. Right away we were a big hit. We went to classes, and she got to know where the different rooms and buildings were on campus. She was able to go from the library to the arts building, where I had all of my classes. It was a pretty campus with lots of trees. It had a quad, and we learned our way around it. During my first semester I took three classes, and she was a big hit with my classmates. She would lie by my side, and I would pet her during the lecture. She really felt at home in the college setting. I enjoyed myself also. She made many friends on campus. She was funny. If she liked you, she would be your friend for life. If she didn't like you, she would ignore you or growl at you. I had to correct her when she did that. I always knew when a friend was approaching on campus. She would wag her tail and howl at them like she was talking to them. One day she did it in the library when someone came over to say hi. People laughed when they heard her. It was not a sound associated with that setting.

We took a few trips into the city, and she was great. People would remark at how well she did and how she would handle the traffic when we would walk on the streets. I took a trip with some college friends at Christmastime to see a show. We had to cross Broadway to get to a restaurant that we were going to eat at. She handled it like a pro.

This was in December of 1970, so we were really becoming a smooth working team. That is how long it takes.

I went to Suffolk Community College for two years. During that time we took another flight to Syracuse to take a course at the university during the summer of 1971. She did great. It was during that summer that I took a trip on a Greyhound bus. I visited the classmate from the Seeing Eye who lived in Binghamton, New York. Sandra enjoyed that also. She just lay under the seat and was very quiet. In the middle of my second year I had to start thinking where I would transfer to for college. After doing research, I decided that George Peabody College in Nashville, Tennessee, would be the one to go to. I started in September of 1972. This was going to be quite an adventure.

As I mentioned before, these dogs had their own personalities. I found out by accident that she liked ice cream and pancakes. My mom would go into the freezer all day long, but when she took the ice cream out, Sandra always knew. One morning my mother was making pancakes, and she gave Sandra some that were left over on a plate. She really loved them. Thereafter, when we had pancakes she would come out to have some. She knew my mom was making them.

Peabody days

I first heard about Peabody College from a counselor friend who told me about it in March of 1972. My mother and I went to the library to do research on it. We got the address and sent for an application. They sent the application with all of the necessary paperwork. We decided to go down and visit around the end of April. We flew down on the thirtieth of April to be exact. Sandra worked like a champ. She behaved on the plane, and when we got to Nashville it was beautiful; full spring and very pretty. All of the flowers were out and were very fragrant. Sandra liked walking around the area where we were staying. There were a lot of colleges, and we were going to visit Peabody. The next day we visited the beautiful campus. We took a tour and Sandra did great.

We flew home later that day, and I was able to go back to Suffolk and finish the semester. We would start in late August.

During that time I went with a group of friends to New York for an overnight stay in a hotel. We went to a Broadway show, ate out in a fancy New York restaurant, and went to church at St Patrick's. Sandra did well in the big city. There was a lot of traffic, which she handled okay.

I relaxed that summer while waiting to go to Peabody in August. I had to learn the area where the college was so I could get around, and Sandra was a big hit with the other students. I explored the neighborhood where the campus was; there were a lot of places to shop and eat if you wanted. We crossed a lot of streets and worked through a lot of traffic situations. One place that we would go to was a steak house across the street from the campus. You could smell them cooking the steaks anywhere on campus. It would make you hungry. To get to the restaurant you had to cross a busy street with a short light. One time I was crossing, and when I was in the middle of the crossing I heard squealing tires. I thought, *This is it.* My life flashed before me, but Sandra stopped on a dime and backed up away from the car that went by. The driver did not stop for the light, and the cops happened to be there waiting for someone to go through the light. They nailed the guy and gave him a ticket. Sandra saved my life.

She got to know the students that I hung around with, and when one of them would come near me she would wag her tail and start barking at them. It was like she was saying hello.

I must say that going to Peabody was one of the more positive times in my life. I met a lot of people who seemed friendly to me. Sandra made friends also.

I mentioned earlier that Sandra loved pancakes. I was at a friend's house one weekend and they had pancakes on a Sunday morning. Sandra began howling, asking for some. The people I was staying with wondered what was happening, so I explained that she just wanted some pancakes; so they made her some. She really enjoyed them.

It was at this time that I had an apartment in the area. I was able to walk from the campus to the apartment. Sandra and I both enjoyed that walk. It was about a mile, and we crossed a lot of streets and walked up and down hills. The apartment was very nice, with a pool that you could swim in during the summer.

I think the most frightening thing that happened to me at Peabody was the time that a tornado spun me and Sandra around on campus. I will always remember the date. It was April 1, 1974. We were having thunderstorms all afternoon. I was walking across the campus. They said that a tornado warning was in effect. It was getting very dark and threatening. Suddenly, the wind began to blow, and it picked me and the dog up and spun us around. We were headed in the opposite direction. A friend came up and told me that a tornado was over the campus but did not really touch down. It touched down east of the campus. That scared me. I got to the dorm and rode out the rest of the storm in the building.

I had been there three years when it came time to graduate. The month before graduation was spent hanging out on the campus remembering my experiences in college. A lot of my friends were graduating with me, so we were all taking that big step of being a college graduate. The big day was beautiful and green, with blue skies. The ceremonies were held on the lawn on the campus. It was a wonderful week for me, full of bittersweet experiences. When my name was called for me to get my diploma, they told me that they had another award for me. I was confused. Then they made an announcement that they were giving Sandra an honorary degree. That was beautiful. I laughed and cried at the same time. It was great. She wagged her tail when she got the degree. That was the end of a beautiful time in my life. We went back to New York to start a new life.

Back home

I now was home, and I missed Nashville at least for the first six months. I went back for a visit a couple of times, but it wasn't the same. I guess that chapter of my life was over. I worked at a school for mentally challenged children and thought about what I was going to do now. I realized after a couple of months that I had to get my master's, so I decided to take a year and relax and work at the school and travel with one of the itinerant teachers who worked in my area. It was nice. The next summer I decided to go to C.W. Post College on Long Island. I would be near home and I could go there on weekends. I could get there by train, and Sandra liked traveling and the work. We moved to another area, which had more sidewalks and was near the railroad station. That was great for me; I could get around easily. I could also get to the station to go to and from school.

I started Post in January of 1977. It was very cold that first week. Snow and ice were on the campus, which made walking a chore. I got through that first week, however, and the next week the snow melted and it was not all that bad. The campus was beautiful. It was an estate that was turned into the college. We did a lot of walking up and down hills. We sure got our exercise. I was there for three years or so, and it was there that I got my first job. But let us not get ahead of ourselves. We had a couple of adventures to talk about.

I noticed that Sandra was starting to slow down. She worked okay, but she did not have that pull like she had when she was younger. She was ten years old and starting to show her age. That summer of 1977 was very hot, and you could tell that it was really getting to her. When I started my fall semester at Post she was really starting to get sluggish. She would have good days and bad days. She still was very gallant in her work. It was in the winter semester. I will always remember the date—February 6, 1978—and one of the worst blizzards that I had ever seen. My friend and I had gone to lunch in the cafeteria, and it was snowing like mad. It was coming down at least three inches an hour. We went to another friend's room after lunch, and then we started back to Brookville Hall where we were living. The snow was up to our knees or higher. In some places it was up to my pockets. It was not only coming down from the sky but blowing up in the wind. There were white-out conditions. We did not know where we were, but Sandra knew. I told my friend that we would go to the first building that she took us to and call security to take us back to the dorm. Sandra took us through the snow. Everything was soundproof, and the wind was blowing through my ears. I thought we would freeze to death. Well, we came to a building. My friend said that it looked like the dorm. Believe it or not, it was. Sandra got us through that snow. I don't know how she did it. I gave her a big hug after that one. Consequently, I did not go out after that experience. I had food in my room, so another friend and I cooked hamburgers in his room. I had the meat and he had French fries. It took a good week for them to get all of that snow cleared from the walks and roads on the campus.

Sandra's last days

I first started noticing that Sandra was starting to fail when I was in New York City attending a meeting. We were taking a bus in Manhattan and she could not get on the bus with me without help. I started getting concerned about that. I had to think of my safety. She went through the rest of the trip okay, but she was slower than she used to be. A couple of months later the vet told me that I would have to think about replacing her. That is a sad thing to hear. You know it is true, but you don't want to believe it. I noticed that she was slower when I went to a convention in Binghamton, New York, five months earlier. She was not keeping up with the other dogs in the group when we would go anywhere. She also looked tired, or so people told me. It was in March of 1978 and I had to make a decision before that summer. I called the Seeing Eye and we talked about it. They sent me a form for the replacement. I noticed as I walked around the campus that she was getting slower and slower.

Other people noticed it also. Her back legs were deteriorating. She had a hard time going up and down stairs in the buildings. People would tell me that I had to think about replacing her. I signed up for a class that would convene on June 17 of that year. I had to find a home for Sandra.

I worked with her the best I could until the end of the semester. Her heart was in it, but her legs could not do it anymore. I still had to find a place for her to go before I went back to Morristown. A friend of mine finally came through just before Memorial Day. I was staying with my cousin and uncle after the semester ended until I went to the Seeing Eye. I brought Sandra to my friend's house on June 10. It was a sad day. She seemed to take it well and accepted retirement without any trouble. I think she was relieved that she was finished working. I was now ready to go back to Seeing Eye to get another dog.

Chapter 2 Misty the Ham

Getting acquainted with Misty

I was looking forward to June 17, 1978. This was the day when I would go back to Morristown to get my new dog. What would its name be? What would the dog be like? All those questions went through my mind as the day drew closer. It was a Saturday and it was pleasant, not too hot. The campus was just as I had remembered it. It was always very nice. I met my instructor, who was young and had been there a couple of years. He took me to my room, and I got settled in. My mom and aunt drove me out from Long Island. We looked around the building again, and I remembered it. After that I settled my accounts with the school. I had to pay fifty dollars this time. My mom and aunt then left, so I went back to my room and unpacked my things.

We had lunch after that. They had the hamburgers again like last time. I wondered what my new dog was going to be like. After lunch I went with the instructor for the Juno walk. A couple of times I called Juno Sandra. The instructor told me that this was normal and that I did very well.

I then met my roommate. He was a first-timer from Philadelphia, so I would be good for him because I had been there before and could show him the ropes.

About six we had dinner, which was good. The class was all together, and the instructor introduced us all. After dinner we had a meeting where we were told about the next couple of days and what would happen. I had been there before, so I knew what to expect. We were given the leash and other equipment we would use with the dog. For me it was familiar. However, I had that excitement, wondering what the new dog would be like.

The next morning we got up about seven and had breakfast. All of the students were excited about the dogs they would get. A couple of us had been there before, so we told the newcomers what it would be like. After breakfast Dick Crocus, the director of training at that time, met with us in the main lounge. He told us about the house rules and how the class would go for the next couple of days. We then went into town with the instructor and had another Juno walk, this time on the streets of Morristown. It was overcast but pleasant, and the walk was nice. The instructor looked at my walking speed and was able to come to a decision about a dog for me.

After the walk the instructors disappeared to have the meeting with the director of training. This is where they come to a decision about the dog you will get. We got together just before lunch, and the instructor told us about our dogs. I was going to get a malamute and German shepherd mix named Misty. I wondered what type of dog she would be. Would she be friendly or reserved like Sandra? Sandra would only let me pet her for a few minutes and would go and lie down where she would not be bothered. I hoped that this dog was more affectionate. We would see.

After lunch we went back to our rooms to wait for the dogs. I told my roommate that this was very familiar. He told me that he was excited about it. It was about two o'clock on Sunday, June 18, 1978. Then the instructor came to the room and asked my roommate to come out to the lounge with him. He was gone a couple of minutes, and then he came back with his dog. The dog was excited, and he did not know what to do. The instructor helped him with that. Then it was my turn. I went into the lounge and sat down on the couch. He then told me to call Misty. I did, and she came over to me, jumped in my lap, and started licking my face. This was so different from when I got Sandra. The instructor said, "That is what I like to see." She kept licking my face and wagging her tail. I brought her back to the room, and we got acquainted. She licked my face for two hours. She wagged her tail a lot. She had a tail that curled up when she wagged it. I did not know about malamutes, so I would have to learn about them. We spent the next couple of hours getting to know each other. I petted her, and she licked my face and hands. She was sure affectionate.

We then went to the lounge and brought the new dogs with us. That went well. Misty was certainly friendly. The instructors took the dogs outside to let them take care of their needs. At 5:45 we went down to dinner and the dogs lay under the table. After supper I hung around the lounge with the other students while we talked about how the dogs were when we got them. Misty liked to lick my hand or my face. About eight we took the dogs outside to the park for the first time. They did very well, and it brought back memories of when I first took Sandra outside. I went to bed shortly after that, because we had to get up early the next morning. My roommate and I talked about what would happen during the next couple of days.

The next morning about 5:30 Misty woke me up by licking my face. I thought she had to go out, but she just wanted to say hello. Then the instructor came by and brought their food; they were using the dry food, which was much better than the canned food that I had to give Sandra. After they ate we took them out to the park area. I could smell bacon cooking in the kitchen. That was nice. After the dogs did what they had to do we came in and got ready for the day. I wondered how Misty would work in town.

After breakfast we took our first walk. She did great. She had a good pull. I was told it was because she was a sled dog that pulled sleds in the Arctic. That was interesting. The walk went well; Misty was turning out to be a good worker. She enjoyed what she was doing. That afternoon we walked the same route that we took that morning along Maple Avenue. There is a tree in the middle of the sidewalk, and Misty took me around it with no problem. It was a hot day, so when the other group did their walk we sat on the grass outside the van. We started to do the South Street route later that first week. We would solo the route on Saturday. We prepared for the solo starting Thursday afternoon. It was quite hot, but we got through the practice okay. Saturday was warm but pleasant.

We did the solo. I discovered how Misty would react around strange dogs. She wanted to visit, and she started whimpering like she was saying come play with me. I had to correct her to keep her focused. The solo went fine, and we came back and had ice tea or coffee at the school. They still had the coffee break at ten in the morning.

That afternoon, my uncle, cousin, and my uncle's mother came by to visit. They were really impressed with Misty. She was very good looking and had nice markings.

That evening after dinner we hung out in the patio area and talked about the first week. It was pleasant and we all had a good time. After the park time we had pizza, which was very good. I was glad that they still did that.

The next day was Sunday, and my roommate and I went into town with our dogs to give them a short walk. Misty enjoyed that. We had a cookout later that evening, and the instructors' families came by and visited with us.

On Monday we started the Elm Street route. This was the route where I had a bad day on the solo when I was there before. The first afternoon it rained, but we got through it okay. Tuesday was hot and humid and I was sweating when I finished the walk. This was in the morning. When we drove back to the campus we could smell honeysuckle along the side of the road. That was pleasant. The afternoon trip was very hot, but Misty handled it fine. Wednesday we had the solo on the Elm Street route. There was a spot where a tree limb was hanging over the sidewalk. We had encountered this before, and during the solo Misty went around it very well. One of the staff was stationed there, and Misty said hello to that person when she went past. That afternoon we started practicing the high school route, the longest route in the series. We worked on that Wednesday afternoon and on Thursday and Friday. We had the solo on Saturday morning, and Misty worked it like a champ. When I would praise her she would wag her tail, which curled up like a malamute. It would tickle my arm; I had to get used to that.

After the solo we had coffee at the school and they told us how we did. We all did very well, and we relaxed the rest of the day. Some people had guests that afternoon, and we had pizza that night. On Sunday morning, my roommate and I went into town to have a little walk, and we had a cookout that evening. The next day we started going into stores and different places to give us the experience of working the dog in various settings.

That week was the Fourth of July, and we had a picnic on the grounds. It was nice and made the holiday enjoyable. On Thursday of that week the retrains went home. I had to stay a couple of more days because my parents could not pick me up until Saturday afternoon. During that week we took a couple of bus rides, which gave the dogs that experience. We also took a local train, because I would be doing that a lot where I lived. On Friday we went into New York to take the subway. Misty was great doing that. I was glad, because we would be doing it periodically. She found the door and took me on the train.

As I said earlier, on Saturday afternoon my parents came to pick me up. It was time to bring Misty home. I was staying with my mother in her apartment until I went back to college in September. Misty would get a lot of elevator work and she would be in an area that had a lot of traffic. I would also get a chance to take buses with her.

When I got home I got Misty acquainted with the park area that I would be using while I was there. We also learned how to get around the building. This was important to get her patterned to the area. I would start working her around the neighborhood in a couple of days.

Bringing Misty home

Well, I had Misty in the apartment and she acclimated to the surroundings very well. I loved the outdoors but could not go out in the yard right away. I had to learn where the benches were in the complex. The first day after I got home my mother showed me different things. We learned where the relief area was and also where the outdoor benches were so I could hang out outside on a nice summer day. The building had an elevator in it, so Misty got work in that environment.

The first week I walked around the block, which had a lot of environments on it. One street was residential, one had office buildings for doctors and was a little busier, and one street was very crowded with stores on it like a city. I would go to Radio Shack and a bakery to give her experience in a store. There was a coffee shop on the next block where I would get coffee or something to eat just like in Morristown. She liked working around the neighborhood and was very accurate. I worked with her in the neighborhood for a couple of weeks, and we took car trips on the weekend to different places.

During the first week in August I took my first trip to the college I would be going to in the fall. We took a bus to Hicksville station and got another bus to Post College. She did that trip very well, and I had to teach her the layout of the campus. She started to get the hang of the area; I knew we would be going back there a couple of times before the start of the semester. She enjoyed the campus, and I introduced her to various people whom I knew.

Back to school

It got to be September and time to go back to college. I was glad to be back where I knew where I was going. Misty liked my dorm room, and I began to find out what type of personality she had. It takes us about six months to really get to know the new dog. I found out very quickly that she was a scavenger. I had a small hot plate in my room for boiling water. I boiled some eggs for salad I was going to make the next day. I left the room for a while and had Misty stay in the room while I did laundry. When I came back she had eaten the hardboiled eggs and the shells that I left on the refrigerator. Sandra never touched them when I left them. I learned that Misty was going to get into things like that. I also found out that she liked to lie on the bed with me while I was relaxing, watching television, or studying. During that first month she wanted me to rub her belly. Sandra would not let me do that for six months.

As I said earlier, I had to teach Misty the campus. I was going back to the dorm from the main quad one day and she got me lost on some grass near the chapel building. A lot of paths converge in that area, and she did not know which one to choose. I was spoiled with Sandra. She could do it automatically. I had to pattern Misty to the area, which I did with practice.

I found out how accurate she was when we went on the subway in New York. When the train came in she went right to the open door and took me on it. That was great. I did not know how she would do in that environment. She was there only once before when I was in training. She remembered, though, and did well. She knew where the door was on the train, and once on she found me a seat. I was glad to see that she was doing so well. She really loved the city and crossed the streets very accurately.

As I mentioned before, she was a scavenger. That day when we were in the city we went to a very fancy steak house. She decided to help herself to a steak, which was on a steam table right at nose level. One of the waiters with a very proper English accent informed me that my dog ate one of the steaks. I was embarrassed and offered to pay for it, but he said that it was okay. The staff in the restaurant got a kick out of it, and when we went to pay the bill and leave they invited us back. The head waiter told me to bring Misty back with me and they would have a steak for her. When she took the steak it happened so fast I didn't know it. I had to expect this with her, because they test you to see what they can get away with.

It is amazing the personality that each dog has. A couple of weeks after the steak episode we went to stay in a hotel where I ran a convention. There she decided to steal candy from a bowl that was in the lobby. I corrected her for that, and she was not happy about it. She did well in the hotel. She learned where my room was, but she liked to take me to

33

the bar in the lobby. I wonder if she was trying to tell me something. Sandra never did that. But Misty had a sense of humor. I liked that. Everyone seemed to like her.

When we get the dogs we have to leave them at home once in a while. After I was in the dorm for a month I left Misty in the room for an hour while I did laundry. She got mad about that and emptied the trashcan all over the room. I was not happy about that. She really wanted to be with me and let me know. I scolded her for doing that, but she went under my bed, which was her favorite place.

I found out by accident that she liked dog toys and tennis balls. I was visiting a friend who also had a dog, and Misty started playing with a tennis ball. We had tennis courts near the dorm, so I found her one that was discarded by a player, and she loved it. She would chase it around the room and have a good time with it. She would bring it to me and I would throw it and she would fetch it.

It soon became winter, and I found out how efficient she was in the snow; her breed of dog was sled dogs, so she loved the snow. Her coat would get very thick, so she was ready for the cold weather. That was great. Anyway, the first year she really did very well in the snow. She would wag her tail and was very happy. I was glad about that, because I needed a dog that would get around the campus when it snowed.

As I mentioned before, she liked to scavenge in the trash and things. One time we left her at home when we went out to dinner. When we came back she had taken the boots and shoes out of the closet. She seemed proud of what she had done. She had a proud look on her face and was lying in the stack of shoes that she made.

I found that she loved kids a lot. She would take me out of our way so she could say hello to children on the street corner or in a store. We were really getting close and she wanted to be with me at all times. When I would wake up in the morning she would be next to me on the bed. She did this a lot in the winter when it was cold. That first Christmas she received a toy that we could play tug of war with. She really enjoyed that. I found that she was a lot more playful than Sandra was.

That first year we were together I got my first job at Post College. I enjoyed that because it was near my dorm and I could get to work on time. Eventually I got an apartment and Misty had to learn a new neighborhood, which she did with no trouble. She was a big hit with the kids in the area. After I had her a year we took our first flight, to a convention in Buffalo. She did very well on the plane. She was very quiet and enjoyed the experience. Later on I took her on another trip to my old college where I had to attend a conference. She was a big hit with the people I hung around with and was very playful.

The job went okay for a year or so and I enjoyed the new apartment. Working in a college was fun, and Misty hung out in the office. I did a lot of talks to school kids in the area and scout troops. The kids were very interested in how the dog worked. I would always give them a chance to pet and play with her. She really enjoyed that. When my job ended at Post I worked at another college for a year's contract, and Misty went with me to work. I would get a ride or take the bus to the school. Misty would know the route to the bus stop and where we had to go. She would always enjoy her work and be glad to go with me when I had to go somewhere.

A couple of horse stories

About a year and a half after I got Misty, I discovered that she loved horses. I was in New York one day on business and I was crossing the street. When I got to the other side she started taking me down the sidewalk like she was going around something. She then started wagging her tail and I noticed that I was next to a horse—one of those horses that pulls a carriage that people ride in. She really enjoyed saying hello. After that when she saw a horse she would bark at them. The bark sounded like she was talking. It was funny to hear that.

Another time we were at a restaurant called the Milleredge Inn. It was set up like a sixteenth-century village with shops in the complex. They had a big plastic horse in front of one of the shops. Well, Misty saw the horse and became very excited. She started pulling me toward it. My girlfriend told me that it was a plastic horse, so I thought I would let her go over and sniff it. When she did she got a perplexed look on her face. My friend laughed when she saw the dog's face. She said that she wished she had a camera. Misty's expression was priceless. She walked away from that horse shaking her head. She just didn't know what to do about that one.

Another horse story happened in New York at Rockefeller Center at Christmastime. I was with my girlfriend and her family and we were visiting the tree. There was a lot of traffic, both vehicular and pedestrian, in the area. We were going to cross the street, and Misty started making that howling sound like she was talking to something. My friend told me that there was a police horse across the street. Everyone on the street corner started laughing because Misty was talking to the horse, and the horse started whinnying back at her. They had a real dialogue going. I then took her across the street to say hello to the horse. The police officer was laughing also. They got acquainted and had a good time. She really loved those horses. Another time I was in Syracuse, New York, where I lived and she saw another police horse in town. As usual she wanted to go over and say hello. When she did the horse was very good to her. The horse somehow knew that Misty was not going to hurt him. Every time after that when we would see that horse the policewoman would say hello and wish us a good day.

A trip to Arlington National Cemetery

Misty was sure a great dog. She would always know how to act in a particular situation. One time we went to Washington, DC, for a visit. We visited Arlington National Cemetery and witnessed the changing of the guard at the Tomb of the Unknown Soldier. She behaved very well.

During the ceremony she sat erect like she knew what was going on. She behaved better than some of the people who were there. Arlington National Cemetery is such a quiet place. It is set on a hill with woods around it to keep out the traffic noise in the area.

Meeting a celebrity

She was as good as all of my dogs were when she met people. One time I was on a flight from Dallas to New York. I met Doc Severinson, the band leader on *The Tonight Show* at that time. This was in 1985. He wanted to give her some of his food, but I had to explain that Misty was working and could not be fed. She always rose to the occasion.

A trip to Williamsburg, Virginia

Later that year in August to be exact, I won a trip to Williamsburg, Virginia. I was doing my internship, and the agency I was working at had a raffle for fundraising purposes. I reluctantly spent a dollar on a ticket, thinking I hadn't a chance of winning. I put it out of my mind. One morning the person who gave me a ride picked me up and told me I had won the raffle. You could have knocked me over with a feather. I won the trip to Williamsburg.

I went with friends for a couple of days. We had a good time seeing all of the attractions. Misty got to see a couple of horses, which she enjoyed very much. When they demonstrated the cannons she jumped a little at the noise but kept her cool for the most part. The hotel where we stayed was very fancy. It was the nicest hotel in the area at that time. We had a lot of good food. One meal we had at one of the taverns in the town, and the next night we ate at the hotel. That meal was sure fancy. We had a lot of nice memories on that trip.

Crazy house

In July of 1986 I went to my brother's wedding in San Jose, California. While we were there we visited the Winchester House, a house that had half-steps and doors that went nowhere. I really had to trust Misty in that setting. I would hear voices and try to tell her to go toward them, but that was not the way to go. There was just a rail or a window. A lot of the passages were zigzag, and I really had to pay attention to her signals, what she was telling me through the harness. We really got a good workout that day.

I worked with her for another four years or so. Along with horses she also loved children. She would know when kids were interested in her. I would go to schools and speak to the students about Seeing Eye dogs and how they work. She would want to play with the kids when we would visit. I would take her harness off and let the kids play and pet her during the lecture. She enjoyed that, and the kids also had a good time.

I had a job as a counselor, and she would always know when the kids were feeling uneasy. She would go over to them and give them her paw or lick their hand or face. This made them feel better, and we were able to get the work done we needed to do.

It was when I had Misty that I went to graduate school. She was with me when I went to classes and when I did my internships. We were there two years, and when I graduated she led me up to the platform to receive my degree. The people gathered there applauded us and she wagged her tail. She somehow knew what was going on.

I noticed around that time that she was getting on in years. She was slowing down and starting to lose her hearing. I had to take it easy with her. That summer I went to a convention in Los Angeles, and it took a lot out of her. She was not well when she got home. She still had good spirits, though, and she enjoyed doing her work.

That fall I moved to Syracuse, New York, and she had to help me learn a new area. We had been there before, so she knew the layout of the city. This was good. The winter up there took a lot out of her. She was eleven years old but still did what she had to do. She still enjoyed the snow because she was a malamute.

That summer we went to the park once a week, and when I would go on the swings she would lie nearby and relax.

End of an era

I had Misty for another year. I noticed that she was slowing down and losing her hearing. This was getting dangerous. I was afraid that she would not react fast enough in an emergency, so I decided to retire her in the beginning of 1990. She worked right up until the end. The last night she was around I made popcorn and gave her some. She really loved it.

The next morning about 6 AM she was sleeping by my bed in her usual spot. I heard her whimper like she was in pain, and then the room got very quiet. I patted her and noticed that she had wet herself. I told her that she had to get up so I could clean up the rug, but she did not move. Something was wrong. I waited for about an hour, and then I realized that she had died. I had never seen anything die before, so I didn't know what had happened. I got this strange feeling: This is permanent. You can't reverse what happened. I was in shock. I didn't know what to do. I had this idea to keep her for a couple of days until I could figure out what to do with her. At around nine I called a friend and she said that she would come right over. When she got to my apartment she confirmed what I feared. I told her that I would keep Misty for a couple of days, but they told me that I could not do that. We contacted another friend, who told us that we could bury her in their yard. So that is what we did. When we put her in the ground I patted her until the hole was filled and I had to take my hand off her. I was crying. It was the worst day I ever had. I had to call the Seeing Eye to see about getting another dog. Misty died on a Saturday, and I called them the following Monday.

She was quite a dog. Her personality was so friendly, and she was liked by so many people. Those were eleven wonderful years.

I went through a grieving process after Misty. I found that I was depressed and angry, but eventually I accepted that she was gone. Upon reflection, I was glad I was with her until the end.

Chapter 3 Bouncy Belle the Bedbug

Getting to know Belle

I had to wait about four months before I could get another dog. I went back to Morristown on February 24, 1990. It was snowing when I got there, which I knew would be interesting, because the streets of Morristown would be icy.

The instructor I had this time was an apprentice whom they wanted me to work with because I had experience with dogs. We did the Juno walk on campus out in a light snow. That was interesting. They had a new way of holding the leash around your wrist. The next day I would know who my new dog would be.

I didn't sleep all that well, because my roommate snored like crazy.

The next morning was very blustery and cold. The sidewalks had a little ice on them. We went in the van to town. They had blankets for us to put over us while we were waiting to go on our Juno walk. The wind was really blowing, and I wondered what I was doing there at that time of year. Two weeks earlier I was in shorts in San Antonio, Texas. I was going to be moving back to Syracuse in a few months, so I guess this was good training for me.

I finally went on the walk in the wind. The sidewalk had ice on it. I was sure glad I didn't throw out my boots. After the walk we went back to the school to thaw out.

We had lunch and we started getting excited. After lunch the instructors gathered us in the Eustis Lounge, the one named after the founder of the school, and they told us what dogs we would get. I was getting a female, a black Labrador retriever named Belle. I asked another instructor who was there if she knew Belle, and she told me that she was sweet natured. That was good.

We then went to our rooms to rest and wait to receive our dogs. My roommate got his dog first; his dog was quiet but moved around a lot. It was finally my turn. It was three months since I had a dog, and I was excited. I sat on the couch, and the instructor told me to call Belle. I did and she came to me and licked my hand and gave me her paw. I got tears in my eyes because I was so glad to have a dog again. I then brought her to my room and we got acquainted. She let me pet her and wagged her tail. I found out that labs wag their tails a lot. This is the first one that I had.

We stayed with the dogs in our rooms until about five, and then we had a meeting in the lounge with all of the instructors. The instructors then took them out to the park area while we waited in the building. We were going to take them out later that evening.

We then had supper and hung around until eight, when it was time to take them out in the wind and cold. There was ice out there, so you had to watch your footing. I was glad I had my winter coat. I was going to move back to Syracuse, New York, from San Antonio, so I didn't want to throw my coat away. I would need it up there.

After we were finished outside we came in and hung around in the lounge. At ten I went to bed so I would be asleep when my roommate came into the room. I put Belle on her night chain and went to bed. I petted her, and she wagged her tail. When my roommate came in she barked at him. So much for getting to sleep before he did. I was tired, so I slept okay even though he probably snored.

The next morning we got up before daylight and went out in the cold again. It must have been five degrees out there. When I came in I took a hot shower to thaw out. We then had breakfast, which was great. It was time to go for that first walk in town with Belle.

Inasmuch as Dianne, the instructor, was an apprentice, she had to work with Doug Roberts, who was director of training at that time. We walked on the sidewalks of Morristown, which had some ice on them.

Belle did okay for her first time out. We then came back to the school to get warm.

By the next Saturday we were ready to do our first solo. Belle and I worked with another student, and we did great. This was the South Street route, which I was familiar with. It was March 2, so the weather was a little chilly. We did the solo okay and got back to the school in time for coffee. The rest of the day we took it easy.

That afternoon Dianne showed Belle and me how to walk on the leisure path. They were constructing an extension to the Eustis Lounge, so we had to go another way than usual. We did okay and were able to go to the gazebo as usual when and if we would have a nice day. It was getting colder and windy, and I knew I would not go out much that day.

On Monday we started the Elm Street route for our next solo. This would take place on Wednesday. Belle and I did the first two tries very well. She was a real trouper. I was glad that she worked out so well.

Tuesday morning it was snowing, which made walking the route tricky. The sidewalks were snow-covered and slippery. I had to watch my footing. However, I got through the two practice trips without any incident. After the afternoon trip I just hung around the school building and read a magazine. Belle was getting used to me. She wagged her tail when we were out on the trips today. That was nice.

The next morning we had the solo, and the sidewalks had a lot of ice on them. One of the blocks had a steep hill on it. I approached the hill; it was icy. I started sliding down the hill while Belle kept walking. I thought I was going to fall and was a little scared. I did not want to break anything. Luckily one of the instructors came up behind me and grabbed my arm to stop me from sliding. I had Belle sit, and we got our composure back. Luckily I had good boots on, which helped me grip the ice. After that the solo went well. I hoped that it would get warmer, which it did the next week; but we are getting ahead of ourselves. The weather was a little warmer, so the ice melted, thank goodness. We would have the solo on Saturday. I was looking forward to that, because that was the last solo in the class. Belle did great. She had her training on the route, so she knew where she was going. She liked to wag her tail when she worked with me, which surprised my instructor, who told me that she never wagged her tail for her.

We had the solo that Saturday, and it was a lot warmer than the other solo. That was a relief.

I spent the rest of the day relaxing, and I walked the leisure path on the campus. That evening we had pizza after we took the dogs outside.

The next day my brother came to visit. It was a warm day, so we went out on the leisure path and sat in the gazebo with some other students and their guests. This was the start of my last week in class, and I would be going back home on Thursday. Belle was doing fine. She was so spirited and lively. She loved to lie in the sun, which I discovered when she would lie in the sun that shone in the window of my room.

The next day I took a train and a bus to give Belle that experience. The following day a couple of us were going to go to New York. I was looking forward to that, because I was from that area. In the afternoon we went to a supermarket and a department store. Belle did well in those places.

As I said earlier, we went to New York the next day. We took the subway and walked the streets. It was sure crowded with a lot of traffic. Belle was fine. We went to Penn Station, which I used to go through every day when I worked in the city and lived on Long Island. It sure brought back good memories. We then went back to Morristown and got ready for lunch. The day was very warm, which was a big switch from when we started the class a couple of weeks earlier. In the afternoon we went to the mall for escalator training with the dogs. Belle was fine with that. I found that she had nerves of iron, which was good for what we were going to be doing. The next day there were numerous lectures. They were held after the walks, and that evening we had prime rib for dinner. That was good. I was going back to San Antonio, Texas, until my apartment was ready back in Syracuse, New York. That would happen a couple of months from then; more about that later.

The next morning my roommate got up very early because his flight was early. I was able to sleep until the regular time to get up. We got up and took the dogs out, and then I packed to go home. A bunch of us left late in the morning and went to the Newark airport where we would catch our flights home. Belle was very good; this was going to be her first flight. Dianne and I waited for the flight to be ready for boarding. She took me on the plane and we said goodbye. She gave Belle and me a big hug, and I could tell that she was proud of us and what we had accomplished in the class. I told her that I hoped I was a help to her when I shared my experiences. She told me that I was. She left me, the plane took off, and we were headed back to Texas for only a few months, when I would move back to Syracuse. I was looking forward to that.

I mentioned earlier that Belle was bouncy. I found out how bouncy she was when we got home. My friend whom I walked with before I went to the Seeing Eye met me when the plane arrived in San Antonio. We went to the apartment, and he left to get me some takeout chicken for supper. I chained Belle to the couch, and she sniffed everything. She could smell Misty even though I had the apartment cleaned. When my friend came back she jumped up on all fours as high as my shoulder, which I found hard to believe. She acted like a kangaroo. That night it sure felt good to get back in my own bed. I didn't miss that roommate snoring. Belle slept on her chain right by the bed.

The next day I took Belle out in the complex and to the grocery store so I could pick up supplies. She did quite well. I noticed that when I would tell her "let's go outside" she would find her way out of the store or any other building for that matter.

We then started doing routes around the neighborhood, which she enjoyed. One street that we walked on was very busy. She found the stores and restaurants that I would go to. I was just biding my time until I would go back to Syracuse.

When I had had her about three months we went to Charlotte, North Carolina, to visit a friend. She worked on the plane very well. I noticed that Charlotte had a lot of trees. The air smelled like the woods, which was very nice. We walked around my friend's neighborhood, and Belle was great. She met some people there, and whenever she would see them she would jump up on all fours up to my shoulder. That's how I knew they were around. We rode the buses a lot there, and Belle enjoyed that. She would always find me an empty seat. I was impressed with that. After a few days we went back to San Antonio; it was hot because it was June.

I spent the rest of the summer just working her around the neighborhood and going to the pool in the apartment. She loved the sun and got plenty of it in that area. One day I could not find her in the apartment. I thought she got out and went into a panic. I found her lying by the window with her head in the sun between the two drapes. I had closed the drapes to keep the hot sun out, and she had put her head between the two drapes so she could enjoy the sunshine. That was funny.

I stayed in San Antonio until October. I then went back to Syracuse. I was glad to get back up there. It was sure a lot cooler, just like fall. That was nice. What a difference from San Antonio. Anyway, I was back home, so to speak. I had to get reacquainted with the area so I could show Belle. She caught on quickly. I spent the next couple of weeks getting things for the house, like new furniture and other necessities. I also spent time with the friends whom I had left when I moved out a year and a half before.

Remember when I said that Belle loved the sun? Well, when the sun shone in the apartment she would follow it right across the living room. It would start on one side of the room and end up right near the couch. It did feel good sitting in its warmth. She was funny that way.

Syracuse gets a lot of snow in the winter. Belle had to learn to negotiate through the snow. It is called the blind man's fog inasmuch as it makes everything soundproof. It is hard to tell where you are at times because everything feels the same. Belle thought it was a game. She loved walking through the deep snow. The first big snow happened just before Christmas. A white Christmas was not just a dream that year. I would be spending Christmas in Syracuse going to a friend's house. My friends and I exchanged presents and I made Christmas cookies. It was great. Belle received presents also.

That year they opened a new mall in Syracuse, one that had a carousel in it. A friend of mine loved riding the carousel, so Belle and I went with him one day. I found out that when dogs ride those types of things they will become dizzy. Evidently they do not know how to look at a stationary item, which prevents this. When we were finished riding she was stumbling around the mall like she was drunk. The operator told me that she was dizzy and explained what happened. Well, we learn something new every day I guess.

Another day I went to the mall to do some Christmas shopping. They had cookies on a tray at eye level to Belle. While we were walking past, a stack of cookies disappeared, thanks to Belle. I guess she enjoyed that unexpected snack, because she licked her lips for an hour after that.

I started a practice of giving my dogs a Christmas present every year. That first year I gave Belle a rubber ring. I found out that she liked that toy because she had played with a friend's dog's ring when I visited one day. She really enjoyed that ring. She would play tug of war with me for hours with that ring. I had a friend who was a social worker, as was I. She was certified, so she could help me with clients that I had in a group home that I was planning to work for in the new year. She had a guide dog that would come over to visit Belle. When Linda would come to work with me supervising my clients at the Pioneer Home, her dog

Hank would play with Belle and the ring. They would play tug of war. It was really cute seeing them do that.

I noticed in the second summer when I had Belle that she seemed to have allergies. We put her on medication, but she scratched a lot during that time. She would be that way until we had the first frost in the fall. That would be sometime in October. She would be okay until the next summer. I felt bad for her, but after the frost she seemed in better spirits.

That winter I dated a girl who was in a wheelchair. That was an interesting experience. Belle really liked the girl and licked her face because she would be sitting very low in her wheelchair. They got along great. Belle would always jump in the air when she saw her. She would bark also like a greeting.

I also had a person who read to me, and she had three kids. I met her in November, and at Christmas time I went to her house for dinner. The kids were there, and that was fun. Belle really loved those kids. She would lick them and play with them. That was fun for her. I gave the kids a gift for Christmas, which they really enjoyed. Belle and I always made them laugh.

I was trying to find a job in the Syracuse area, but it was quite difficult. I worked with the Center for Independent Living, where I met Ilene, the girl in the wheelchair that I mentioned earlier. The wheelchair created other difficulties for her, as I would come to find out.. We went to a seminar at a hotel where she had to go down in a freight elevator, which bothered me because I was claustrophobic. I did not like small elevators. We had to get down to a seminar room. Belle and I could get there very easily by just walking down the stairs from the lobby in the hotel. But with Ilene I had to go with her and her wheelchair down an elevator and out into a parking lot in the snow. She could not get across the parking lot because there were steps, so Belle and I had to go out in the snow and walk over to the meeting room where a couple of the participants could carry her in her wheelchair over to the meeting room.

I really felt lucky that with Belle I could just walk down the stairs and walk into the meeting room. I guess there are advantages to everything. In other words, the meeting room was not wheelchair accessible.

Anyway, Ilene started coming over to my house. That was great. She was able to get into my apartment with her wheelchair, which was good. When she would come Belle would greet her warmly.

In the spring of 1992 I began to realize that finding a job in Syracuse, New York, was going to be difficult if not impossible. Besides, the winters in Syracuse were very bad. There was a lot of snow, which made getting around with Belle very difficult. I had to go out in all types of weather so that Belle would get her biological needs met. If it was fifteen below I had to go out in it whether I liked it or not. When it was snowing and windy outside it was hard to tell where I was going. Also, the salt on the streets that they put down to melt the snow irritated her paws. I had to move further south where the winters were a little milder. I wanted to go back to Long Island, but it was too expensive there. When I was training with Belle one of the persons in the class told me about Atlanta. He seemed to like it, so I decided to have a look at the area that summer. I also was interested in Raleigh, North Carolina, because some of my friends were thinking of moving there. That spring I had a job interview in the Raleigh area. I went in April. It was beautiful. The area had a lot of trees and you could hear a lot of birds. I really enjoyed that. I didn't get the job in Raleigh, so I concentrated on the Atlanta area. I visited Atlanta in August of 1992 and was impressed with the transportation that they offered. Belle liked it also. I had a friend who lived in the area who had me stay with him. I stayed there for a week, and we took the train and buses a lot. One could travel to many areas of the city. I decided to move there.

I had to endure another winter in Syracuse before I could move there in the following spring. The winter of 1992–93 was one of a lot of snow and bitter cold weather. There was a week when it didn't get above twenty degrees. That was cold. You wanted to stay in the house as much as possible. It would be as cold as ten below in the morning. When I would take Belle out I had to dress in layers so I would not get frostbite. In March of 1993 there was a tremendous snowstorm. We had two to three feet of snow. When I would walk around the area the drifts were over my head. I was glad I was going to be leaving in a couple of months.

The move to Atlanta

I was going to move to an area of the country that was very strange to me. Talk about taking a risk. I would be there for ten years, but let's not get ahead of ourselves. I moved there at the end of April of 1993. This was after there was snow the week before, which was almost depressing. The apartment I was going to move into was small but nice. In the spring you could smell a lot of honeysuckle, which was great. The transportation was also very good in the area. Belle and I liked that. We could learn our way around very easily. The first week I was there I rode the subway frequently. They had a system where you could transfer from the train to a bus without paying another fare, unlike in New York where you paid a fare every time you transferred. When I had visited the area the previous summer my friend introduced me to a girl who lived about forty-five minutes away by train from my house. I learned how to go to that area where she lived with her kids and would go down there periodically.

One of the reasons why I moved to Atlanta was to find a job. There seemed to be more opportunities in that area than in Syracuse. I first had to become established. As I said before, the transportation was great. I was able to go to many areas of the city, which was very convenient. Belle liked it very much. She loved traveling the subways. She knew where to go and learned fast.

As I mentioned before, when she saw someone or people whom she knew she would jump up on all fours. She would jump up to my shoulders. She looked like a kangaroo. So I always knew when someone

I knew was coming. I also found out that she loved Frisbees. When I was down at my friend's house with the kids they were playing with a Frisbee in the yard. Belle jumped for it and caught it in her teeth. She was so happy when she was doing that. I was glad I was able to give her some downtime.

For the next couple of years I went around the Atlanta area on the Marta where Belle worked very well. We were able to go to various parts of the city. I learned how to get around Lenox Mall when a friend of mine was there to visit with me in 1994.

That really came in handy that Christmas when I went shopping for gifts for various people.

During the first summer I was in Atlanta I noticed that her allergies had kicked up again. I brought her to a vet, and they told me that I had to give her a special bath. I did that, but the allergies only got worse. After I was there about a year I took her to a canine dermatologist who told me that I would have to start giving her a vaccine for the allergies that next summer. I had to give her shots, which was awkward. I learned to do it and did the best I could. I started to go to a center to look for a job. I also started volunteering at one of the children's hospitals. This was in the spring of 1995, and I was very busy with that. This was after going on a few interviews and not having success.

A warm place

I belonged to a singles group where we would go out on a lot of social engagements. One place we would go to was the Ritz Carlton Hotel in Atlanta. We would go to the lounge and have drinks; they had a wood-burning fireplace. Belle loved lying by that fireplace. She would stretch out like it was heaven. I enjoyed that fireplace also. It was very cozy sitting in front of it.

I went through the center and learned more computer skills and interviewing techniques. I went on numerous interviews and was able to go to different parts of the state with my counselor. In the fall of 1995 I went with Belle every day to the center in the morning. She knew how to get there from the train station. It was an easy walk, which gave me exercise. One of the bus drivers got to know Belle and would say hi to her when the bus pulled up, so I knew I was on the right vehicle. In November just after Thanksgiving I went to Macon for an interview at the Academy for the Blind. It looked promising, and I left with hope. They called me in for a second interview just before Christmas. The interview would take place in early January. I went to Texas that Christmas and came back just before New Year's in 1996. I was looking forward to the interview just after New Year's. Belle was a smart dog. During the Christmas shopping season I went to Lenox Mall, and she would remember how to get around. She enjoyed the work, and I was able to get my gifts for my family. Earlier that fall I went to Warm Springs, Georgia, for a seminar and we took a walk around the lake that was on the grounds of the rehabilitation center where I was staying. She was really interested in the ducks that were in the lake. She was a black Lab so, and is what they do.

The move to Macon

In January 1996 I had a second interview at the Academy for the Blind. They must have liked what I had to offer, because on January 12 they offered me the position. I was excited about that, because it meant that Belle and I would be moving to Macon. About a week after the offer I went to Macon to look for an apartment. I found one that was right next to the school. In fact, the complex was right behind the campus. That was great, because it meant that I would be able to walk to work. I enjoyed that. I was happy Belle became interested in the area.

We moved on February 7, 1996. I was excited and nervous at the same time. I had to learn a new area, which was a challenge. The moving day was hectic. I moved from a one-bedroom apartment to a three-bedroom with a dining room and kitchen. It was like a house. The apartment also had a sunroom with a lot of windows. I liked to sit there in the morning and have my coffee. Eventually I put a bird feeder outside the window, which made it very pleasant. In the nice weather I would open the windows and a nice breeze would come in.

The day after I moved, a mobility instructor came down and showed me and Belle where the school was and where my office was located in the school building. I had to work in the main office in town, so the next day we learned the bus route to the main office. There was a lot of walking involved in getting around the town, but it was okay because it gave me and Belle good exercise.

On February 16, 1996, I started working at the Academy for the Blind in Macon, Georgia. It was a dream job for me because I could walk to work unless I had to go downtown for a meeting or other business, and I had always wanted to work in a school setting. Belle and I got to know the campus and the kids who attended the school. We both enjoyed the kids; Belle would wag her tail when we would meet one of the students and I would smile and say hello to them and maybe stop and talk. We were both a big hit.

While I was working at the school during that summer I noticed that Belle had her allergies back again. She would get bumps on her skin, which would give off an odor and a fluid would come out of them. This condition would make her uncomfortable. It got worse in the fall for some reason. We had a camp program for kids that summer, and the kids noticed that she had bumps on the skin. I felt bad about that because she was uncomfortable. I took her back to the skin specialist in Atlanta, and they told me that her allergies were really getting bad. We found out that she was allergic to the falling leaves, among other things. The vaccine I was giving her was not working anymore. I was looking at the possibility of getting a new dog in the next year. I hated to do that, but I almost had no other choice—she was suffering so.

During Christmas she developed a tumor on her leg that I had to have removed. I had it done a couple of days before New Year's. This made it difficult for her to walk for a couple of weeks after that.

Meanwhile, the state of Georgia who I was working for had a reduction in force, so I was out of a job. That was mean, because I enjoyed that job very much. The kids also enjoyed having Belle and me.

I had to decide what to do with Belle. Her allergies were getting worse, and it was not a good thing to keep her working. She had the attitude that she did not care because her allergies were such a distraction. It was not an easy decision to make, but I had to send her back and get a new dog. I had to arrange to go back to Morristown to train with a new dog. So on May 22, 1997, I put Belle on a plane for Morristown.

When I got home from the Atlanta airport I called the Seeing Eye to make sure that she was picked up at the Newark airport. Pete Lang called me and told me that she had arrived safely. I had all of the paperwork to go to the Seeing Eye on June 21. I had to wait a month and use a cane to get around. I could use the cane okay, but it was slow getting around. I dealt with it and was looking forward to when I would go back to get my dog.

I had to walk as much as possible before training. You have to do that before you go to the Seeing Eye so that you are used to walking briskly. I did this by walking the track at the school. It is a quarter of a mile around, so I could walk two or three miles and get good exercise.

The day drew closer for me to depart. I had done this before. I had that familiar anticipation of what the new dog would be like and what its name would be. It was time to meet a new friend.

Chapter 4: Murdock, the gentle giant

Getting acquainted with Murdock

It was time to go back to Morristown to get a new dog. This was the fourth time I would be going there, so I knew what to expect. I flew up to New Jersey from Georgia with a friend who was also getting a dog on June 21, 1997. The flight went okay, and we arrived in Newark to take the trip to Morristown. They had a fancy limousine service pick us up. The day was hot, so the air conditioning in the car felt good. We got to the school about one and met our instructors. I was shown to my room and then had lunch.

After lunch we had the Juno walk, and my instructor said that he had a couple of possibilities for a dog. He mentioned that I would find out the next day. We hung around until dinner. The meal was very good, and the whole class was together. After dinner we were taken on a tour of the building.

Since I was there last the school had an expansion program. They added onto the dining room, put in a new Eustis Lounge named after the school's founder, and added new students' rooms onto the building. Every student had his or her own room, thank goodness. I didn't have to put up with anyone's snoring like last time. They also made the main lounge upstairs bigger and put a kitchen in it. They put a computer center in the basement and a grooming area where we could brush the dogs in comfort at any time.

The next morning we went to Morristown for the usual Sunday morning walk with the instructor acting like the dog. That went well, and we got back to the school and got ready to meet our new friends. This happened after lunch.

I went to my room to wait for the call to the lounge to meet the new dog. However, the instructor brought the dog into my room. He told me that he had my dog with him. The dog's name was Murdock. He was a mix between a golden retriever and a Labrador retriever. He was reddish gold in color; very handsome looking. The instructor told me that he was very mature in his work and that he loved New York City. He was very devoted to his master, or so I was told. The instructor left us so we could get acquainted. The dog did not want any part of me at first. I patted him, but he whimpered for the instructor. I realized the task I had ahead of me. It was a long couple of hours, but I got through it. About five we all gathered in the main lounge, and I found out that the girl who came up from Georgia with me had Murdock's sister. That was interesting.

After supper we took the dogs out to the park area, and Murdock did okay. I found that he was very quiet and friendly with the other dogs. I would find out how he works the next day.

The next morning we went into Morristown, and he did very well. The instructor was right; he was very mature in his work. I knew this because he was very confident, which is a skill that has to develop in dogs that are in training. He obeyed me very well, which is another skill that the dogs have to develop with us, because they want to be with the instructor in most cases. I asked the instructor if he was sure that he had not worked with someone else. He told me that he had not. Murdock really knew what he was doing. When I put the harness on him he became very businesslike.

We got through the first week of training without a hitch. That Saturday he did the solo route like a champ.

That afternoon we were shown the leisure path on the campus. This is a path that winds through the grounds and is a half-mile in diameter. Murdock loved walking on that path, and I did also. That afternoon I had visitors from Long Island. My friend told me that she noticed how trusting I was with Murdock compared to the other students that she observed working with their dogs. The next day I went out on the path again with Murdock. I could tell that he was beginning to bond with me. The bond that we develop with our dogs is very important, because we literally have to trust our dogs with our lives.

On Monday of the second week we did the Elm Street route, which was the route where I had the experience with Belle slipping on the ice. I didn't have to worry about that this time inasmuch as it was June. In fact, it was quite hot that afternoon when we were practicing the route. They had lemonade for us in the lounge when we got back from our walk with the dogs. That was good. We soloed the route on Wednesday morning in a drizzle. It almost felt good because we didn't get too hot.

That afternoon we did the high school route, which we soloed a couple of days later on the Fourth of July. We do these routes so we can gain confidence with the dog.

We soloed the route in the morning. Murdock decided to take me out in the street rather than walk on the sidewalk. The instructor brought it to my attention, and I corrected the situation. This was unusual for Murdock.

That afternoon we went to an ice cream shop in Morristown. The ice cream was very good. We were now in the freelance part of the class. This is when we go into stores, on trains and buses, and to other places where we will work the dog when we get home.

That weekend we worked the dogs in a suburban neighborhood where you had quiet streets where families with kids lived. Murdock loved that because the kids reminded him of the people who raised him when he was a puppy.

That Monday we went to an office building in Morristown that had a lot of steps up and down. Murdock worked like a champ. I again asked the instructor if he had been out in the field before. He said no he hadn't. That afternoon we went to a mall to work the dogs on escalators. They developed a technique where we can bring the dogs on escalators and they can get off without getting their paws caught. This is good, because in Atlanta when I would go there I had to ride an escalator that had to be five hundred feet long in the airport and another that is the longest in the world in the Marta train system.

The next day we took Murdock into New York to ride the subways. The trainer told me that he was in New York during his training and he loved it—a man after my own heart, because I loved New York myself. We drove in the van to the Port Authority garage on Eighth Avenue. Murdock remembered where the elevator was from the last time when he was there. Even the instructor was amazed about that. We rode on the subway and then came out to walk the streets. Murdock took me up the stairs and right out onto the street. He did great with the crowds. He took me to the curb, and we crossed very smoothly. He loved it! We walked around the city and went to a New York deli for lunch. That was fun. Needless to say, we had a great day in the Big Apple. We took the subway back to the garage and drove back to Morristown.

It was getting time to take Murdock back home to Georgia. One thing that they did was read us the dog's puppy profile. Murdock was raised by two boys, one thirteen years of age and the other ten years old. He was very playful with his family. He lived on a very busy street in Pennsylvania. They said that his paw got clipped by a truck, which did not bother him when it came to dealing with traffic. I was glad of that. The kids said that he loved toy stuffed animals. I had to remember to get him a couple for Christmas.

That evening we had prime rib for dinner. It was a tradition that the night before the retrains—those who came back for replacement dogs—went home they made a special dinner as a sendoff for us who had dogs before.

Going home with Murdock

The next morning we got up early and I got ready to take Murdock back home with me to Macon, Georgia. We had a light breakfast and headed to the airport. When we got there we took the plane back to Atlanta. Murdock did great on the flight. It was his first plane ride, but it was like he had done it before. We got to Atlanta and then took the ninety-eight-mile trip to Macon where I was living at the time. I showed him around the apartment and got him acquainted with the complex that I was living in. He sniffed everything in the apartment; I guess he could smell Belle's scent on the furniture and in the carpeting.

The rest of that day we just took it easy and I introduced Murdock to the person living with me. When we first bring the dogs home we have to take it easy with them. We have to either keep them on leash or tie them to a sturdy piece of furniture so they get used to the new surroundings. We have to work on the bonding process, which takes on a new dynamic now that we have them at home in our own house. They try to see what they can get away with. They will try everything, such as getting into the trash and going up on the couch and things.

The next day I took Murdock out for a little walk in the neighborhood. I was out for about twenty minutes, and he did great. He sure worked well. It was very hot and humid, so you didn't want to stay out very long. I planned to take it easy on the weekend so he would get familiar with the house and my routine.

A couple of weeks after I got him home I noticed that he had developed a sore on his neck. I called the vet, and when I brought him there they told me that he had allergies. I was not happy to hear that. It was an allergy problem that made me have to give up Belle. The vet started treating the sore, and I contacted the Seeing Eye to determine what to do. He was so good natured, and I hated to see him suffer.

Along with that we were trying to get used to each other. It is a job in itself. It takes a good six months to a year before we are a smooth working team. However, with Murdock, because he was so mature in his work, it happened sooner. We walked around the campus that I worked at. I got a new job shortly after I brought him home, so I had to learn a new route in Macon, from the art center where I would be working to the Y. He picked up on it quite rapidly.

When we bring a new dog home they can get into mischief. One night Murdock knocked over the garbage can in the kitchen. That created a mess, and I had to correct him for it. Another thing he did was one day I made steak on the grill. When I brought it inside he decided to help himself to some. He was a big boy, so he had a large appetite.

I mentioned that he had become very devoted to me. About a month after I brought him home I started working at an art center for children. We had to do various jobs on the grounds of the center. One thing I had to do was weed the garden. It would be hot outside, so I would try to leave Murdock in the air-conditioned building, but he would have none of that. He would go crazy jumping up and down and howling. I would have to come in and get him and bring him out with me. I would tie him to a tree near the place where I was working, and as long as he could see where I was he was content. It could be a hundred out there, but he didn't mind as long as he was with me. That is how devoted he was.

He still had his allergies. He had that sore on his neck, which never went away even in the winter. That was too bad. When I had him home about a month I had to bring him to the vet to get the sore treated. The vet told me it was from the allergies.

As the instructor at the Seeing Eye told me, he was very mature in his work. We would walk around Macon visiting different people who lived in my neighborhood. It was fun, and he enjoyed the work. He really loved doing it. These dogs love their work. It is fun to them. When I would get his harness he would get very excited and wriggle into it.

When the kids were raising him as a puppy they called him the gentle giant. This was because he was so gentle with his toys. He loved stuffed animals. I got them for him the first Christmas I had him. I went to Texas to see my parents, and my mom got him a couple of stuffed bears. He was so gentle with them. He really enjoyed them and walked around the house carrying the toys. I brought them home with me when we left after the holidays. I went back to my job at the art center, where he was a big hit with the kids.

I worked at the center, and Murdock did his job with devotion. It seems that the male dogs are more devoted to their master than the females. Not that the females are not devoted, but the males seem to be more demonstrative about it.

In April I had to go back to Texas because my father passed away. I had to leave Murdock at the house when we went to the funeral, and he had a fit. I left him in my room while I was gone, and he wrecked the place. He got into my luggage and pulled out all of my clothes so he could lie in them. He took the covers off the bed and made a mess of them. He really wanted to be with me. After we got back he stayed with me and was very quiet. They told me when I got him that he was very devoted to me, and he was.

I stayed at the art center until August, and I had a chance to work in the preschool area. That was great. We were a big hit with the kids. We would go to the class and I would sit with the kids during circle time. I would always have a couple of kids sitting on my lap, and they would pet Murdock. He would lie there quietly while they petted him. As long as he was with me he would not mind what the kids did with him. After I finished my contract there in August I would volunteer there once a week with the preschoolers. I would go to their other facility on the city bus with Murdock. He loved riding the buses. He would go to a place one time and remember how to get there when we went again. As they said when I got him, he was really mature in his work.

Mouse hunter

That fall, the apartment I was living in had mice in it. The whole complex was infested with them. I would always know when there was one in the house because Murdock would get excited and for no reason at all run into the kitchen, very curious about what was going on in there. He would not catch the mice. I had to get traps for that.

We finally got an exterminator in the complex to get rid of the rodents. However, Murdock was always on guard for them.

A priest's blessing

In the spring of 1998 I became friends with the pastor of my church. He loved Murdock. I really got to know him when he drove me up to Atlanta so I could catch the flight to go to my father's funeral. When I came back, every time I would go to church he would give Murdock a special blessing. He loved that dog. Murdock could do no wrong in his eyes. When Murdock had the allergy problems he looked into the idea of bringing him to Auburn University in Alabama, which had a good veterinary school. That did not pan out.

In 1999 I took a job at a charter hospital running various groups. I primarily ran them for the kids, and I did the others when I worked on the weekends. Murdock and I learned our way around the hospital, and he really enjoyed being with the patients, especially the kids. He would be very quiet and was a big hit. As long as he was with me he was fine. He would put up with anything as long as he knew where I was and that I was okay. We worked there for a little over a year, and then the hospital closed down and I had to find another position.

That fall I took a trip to LaGrange, Georgia, where I would ultimately live the next year. You could walk to a lot of places in the town, and Murdock loved that. He would be very happy when we would go there and walk around the town. He would handle the traffic very well.

I noticed that during that time Murdock's allergies were getting worse. He would scratch himself a lot and had that sore on his neck that would not go away. He also developed problems with his stomach. The vet told me that the allergies caused it. I had tests done and found out that he was allergic to almost everything growing in Georgia. He had to move to a northern climate. I hated the thought of having to go back to Morristown, but I had no other choice. I also had to find that other position, which I did in June of 2000. It would involve a move to that small town of LaGrange, Georgia, where I had visited the previous fall. I know that Murdock would like moving there.

A move to LaGrange

I made the move in late June, and Murdock did as well as he could under the circumstances. I got into the new job working at a child center where I started out by running various groups. They went very well. Murdock and I were a big hit with the kids.

Remember that I mentioned earlier that he was very devoted to me? Well, he sure was. While running a group one afternoon I decided to leave him in my office where it was cool. He did not like that idea. Somehow he got the door opened and wandered around the center looking for me. One of the counselors got him and put him back in the office. So much for leaving him. I brought him with me to the various groups that I ran. If we did any activities that involved movement around the room and I left him at my desk, he would get very nervous. He always had to be with me. That is devotion.

I found that LaGrange was an easy town to walk around in. Murdock and I got to know the town quite well. However, his heart was not in it because of the allergies. That was unfortunate, because he was a great worker.

One day an instructor came down from the Seeing Eye to work with another student who lived in the area, and she worked with Murdock and me. She told me that he was doing okay, but you could see that the allergies were diminishing his concentration. She said I could keep him, but the allergies were only going to get worse. A vet that I was working with in the area concurred with that opinion. So I had to think about going back to Seeing Eye that fall.

I made application and was accepted for the October 2000 class. Also, the company where I was working was bought out by another company, so I would start working for the new company in October. Murdock was as comfortable as he could be. He seemed to have the allergy problems in the fall and spring. He still had that open sore on his neck that would not heal. The poor guy was miserable. When I contacted the Seeing Eye about the new dog I emphatically told them that I did not want a dog that had allergies. If I got another dog with allergies I would return it and not go back for another one. It was too humiliating.

I went shopping for clothes to take with me to Morristown because it would be fall and the weather would be cool.

It was getting close to the time to go back to Morristown. I would bring Murdock up there with me and drop him off at the school; more about that later.

I started preparing for the trip back to the Seeing Eye. I had to leave the house for three weeks and prepare things for that, like having someone collect my mail while I was gone. I also had to go to work, which took up a lot of my time. On October 28 I would go up there. I hoped it would be a long while before I went back there to train for another dog. I hoped there would be no more allergies to deal with.

Saying goodbye to Murdock

The day I was to leave dawned sunny and cool. Some friends drove me up to Atlanta from LaGrange so I could catch my flight. The Seeing Eye arranged my flight, so everything was set. Murdock was very quiet. I think he knew that something was going on and a big change was about to take place in his life. He was about to take his last plane trip and go into retirement.

The flight was an hour late, because the pilot did not show up. When he finally did we took off for Newark, New Jersey. We arrived without a hitch and met the cab/limousine at the baggage claim area to go to Morristown. Murdock was a real trouper, and he was very quiet. I thought about what was about to happen, and I felt sad and guilty at the same time. Was I doing the right thing?

I hoped so. When we got to New Jersey it was blustery and chilly, typical for late October. It was October 28. I would get the new dog that Monday, which was in two days. I rode with another student who was going for his first dog, a gentleman from Minnesota. I told him what he could expect in the class. He was both excited and anxious at the same time. I was too. They told me that I would be able to spend some time in private with Murdock to say goodbye to him.

We finally arrived at the school. I was happy and sad at the same time. I met my instructor, John Keen. He explained to me that I could take as much time with Murdock as I wanted. I went into one of the offices for about fifteen minutes and gave him a hug. I told him that he was a good boy and explained to him what was going to happen. I started to cry. Separating from him was very difficult. After the fifteen minutes were up they came and took him. I gave him another hug and then he was gone. If it were not for those allergies he would have been with me for ten years or so.

Chapter 5 Nan the silly dog

Getting acquainted with Nan

Well, as I mentioned earlier, it was October 28, 2000, and here I was in Morristown about to get another dog. I did not know who it was, but I hoped that I would have this one a good long time.

After I got settled in, my instructor and I did the Juno walk. It was brisk and cool outside, which was okay for late October. He told me I did well and that he had a few possibilities for me. I was glad to hear that. I relaxed for the rest of the afternoon until supper. I was still feeling let down from Murdock. However, I had to put that on hold so I could psyche myself up for the new dog. I didn't start feeling excited until the next day.

Dinner consisted of turkey and all of the trimmings, and after dinner we gathered in the main lounge for a meeting. We all introduced ourselves and told what dog we were coming for. People were impressed that I was coming for my fifth dog. We had people there from all over the country. This is what makes the Seeing Eye such an interesting place.

There were some changes in the training schedule this time. We were going to get the dogs on Monday instead of Sunday. They felt that this would give the instructors more time to evaluate us and come up with a worthwhile match.

Sunday was chilly and I had to wear a heavy coat when we went into town to do another Juno walk. The instructor told me that I did okay and that he was narrowing his choices for a dog. That was good. When they match us with a dog they take into consideration our life style and walking speed. Some dogs work better in cities while others prefer a quiet environment.

They had an instructor from Australia observing the school and how it works. One of the Seeing Eye's instructors went there to observe their program. When we got to town John and I did another Juno walk. This time we were on the streets where there were real crossings. The instructor from Australia was with us observing how John worked with me. I had had dogs for thirty-two years at that point, so they wanted to tap into my experience.

After lunch the instructor brought dogs into the lounge for us to meet and play with. This is something new that they do before they give us our new dogs. They want to find out how we interact with dogs and make sure that we and our dog will be compatible. We were with the dogs for an hour. We petted and played with them. The dogs showed affection by licking us or giving us their paws; whatever they did to show affection.

After supper we had a lecture where we were told what would happen the next day. We would go on another walk in the morning, and in the afternoon we would receive our dogs. After the lecture we had a wine and cheese party. That was nice inasmuch as we could get to know each other better. There were about four instructors in our class, so there were students from all over the United States and Canada. I then went to bed to get a good night's sleep. The next night I might be awake with the new puppy.

The next morning we got up around six and got ready for the day. It was a crisp late October day. Thoughts went through my mind: What will the dog be like? What will its name be? I would soon find out.

After a good breakfast we took the last Juno walk in Morristown. The instructor told me that he had three possibilities for me. I told him that I was glad to hear that. After the walk we hung around and had a lecture with the executive director. He welcomed us to the school and told us what he did and went over some of the rules. The time for getting the dog was getting closer.

After lunch we went back to our rooms to get ready to meet the new dog. That is always an exciting and anxious time. It was October

30, 2000. As I mentioned, this was a new policy that the school had implemented, giving out the dogs on Monday.

The time finally came around two in the afternoon. The instructor came to the door and had me go out to the lounge. He told me that the new dog was a black Labrador retriever named Nan. I called her and she came over to me. She was very silky for a Lab. I petted her, and she licked my face. I was glad to see that, because it meant that she was curious about me. I took her back to my room, and she whimpered a little. She had to get used to me. I petted her again, and she liked it. I also scratched her ears, which I found were very silky. Her ears were not floppy. She wanted to lie on the floor, so I lay with her to get to know her.

In the past we would not work the dogs in harness until the following day, but this time we took the dogs out on the leisure path in harness an hour after we got them to see how we worked together. The leisure path is a half-mile path that winds around the campus. It is circular so you can't get lost on it. It goes through two gazebos that show you how the dog stops for obstacles.

After the walk I took Nan back to my room and hung around with her until we took them out for them to take care of their biological needs. We then waited until supper and then went with them to the dining room. Nan was very good.

After supper we had a lecture on grooming and were shown the grooming room. It had a bench in it where we could sit and brush the dog. I remembered it from last time when I was there with Murdock. After that we took the dogs outside again, and I went to bed shortly after we came in. The next day was going to be an early one. It was a long day with a lot of stress around getting the new dog. I hoped that Nan would sleep. They told us not to put the dog's rug down the first night until we saw if they would have an accident in the room. Fortunately, that did not happen with Nan.

The next morning we got up about 5:45 to feed and take the dogs outside. Nan slept okay, except that she barked during the night at something that she heard. I didn't hear a thing, but she did. They have great hearing. We came back in and an hour or so later had breakfast.

After breakfast it was time to make the first trip into Morristown and work the dogs. As usual we had a simple walk the first day, and she did great. We went up one or two blocks and doubled back to the van. I noticed that she wagged her tail a lot. That was nice. I also noticed that she is a very soft-natured dog. Dogs are usually hard or alpha or soft-natured, which is when they are very submissive.

After lunch we did the route again. Nan did great. It was fall, and the leaves were on the ground. It was nice walking through the fallen leaves. The instructor took one person at a time out on this short route. While I waited in the van I could feel the warm sun through the open door. It really felt good.

On Thursday we started practicing for the South Street solo. I remembered it from last time when I was there. We were to do the solo on Saturday. That morning we started obedience and keeping them away from food that might be on the floor. We were taught to tell them to leave it so they would know not to touch the scraps on the floor. Obedience makes it clear to the dog that they have to be obedient to us when we ask them to do something like come.

On Saturday we had the South Street solo. We usually work with a partner, but the person I was going to work with was not feeling well so I did the route myself. It was just me and Nan, and we did great. We passed the solo with flying colors.

In the afternoon when we were finished with lunch we were shown the leisure path, which I knew already. Nan really enjoyed going out there. The air was crisp, and it was good exercise when we walked the path. Some of the people had company, and I relaxed for the rest of the day and bonded with Nan by spending time alone with her petting and talking to her.

The next day was Sunday, and we had a priest in our class. He conducted a Catholic mass in the lounge in the school. This was nice for those students who wanted to attend. I found that Nan was very well behaved in a church setting.

The next day we started working on the next solo route: the Elm Street route. As before, it was in a busier section of town, with more traffic.

There were two apprentice instructors hanging around in the building, and they had to wear blindfolds while in the student area. They had dogs with them on leashes. This experience was to teach them what it was like to be in the building as a blind person, their future students. It was probably a real learning experience for them. When I talked with them I asked if it was scary for them, and they said no.

We practiced the route for two days and had the solo on Wednesday. During the solo Nan had to react when a car cut in front of us when we were walking in front of a gas station. They taught the dogs to back up when a car cut in front of them.

Throughout training, the head of training would drive a car around and cut in front of us for what is called traffic checks. The dogs have to be able to handle this situation very precisely. Nan handled it very well.

I was going to be leaving earlier than any of my other classmates because I had to get back to work. One of the field instructors was going to come to LaGrange and work with me. This would be good because I would learn my home area better.

One of the other changes that they made was having us not do the high school route if we did not want to. I elected not to bother with this route. I did want to take the train and the bus because Nan might be doing that with me, especially when I visited Long Island. I went there at least once a year. We took the train and the bus the day before I was slated to leave. In the afternoon we went to a shopping mall to give Nan experience in that environment. After that we took her to the animal hospital that they have on the campus. It is a state-of-the-art facility. She got a clean bill of health. When we were finished doing that we took her to a field that was behind the clinic. We put her on a twenty-foot leash and had her run, and then I called her so she would learn to come when I called. This would be good if we were in a fenced-in yard.

That night I packed to go home with Nan. I was glad I had brought two suitcases, because they gave me a lot of things to take home with me. They gave me some food, a food pan to feed her with, an extra leash and bed chain, and her paperwork. Another thing that we did was go over her puppy profile. She was raised by a fifteen-year-old girl who also had a bird and a cat. She did very well in their home, and she liked tennis balls. The night instructor brought in a cat for us to work on how the dogs would react to that distraction. Nan did not want any part of it. She was very meek. After the cat experience it was time to take the dogs out for the night and go to bed. I had a big day coming up.

Going home with Nan

The day I was to go home with Nan dawned rainy and dark. I was going to Georgia, so I knew it would be warmer there. When we got up to take the dogs outside it was pouring. It was a good thing I had a raincoat. After we came back inside I finished packing and then we went down for breakfast. I would be leaving for the airport later that morning.

After breakfast I said goodbye to the other members of my class and waited for the person who was going to drive me to the airport to make an appearance. He came about 9:30 because my flight was leaving about noon. We loaded the car and went to the airport. Nan was good about riding in the car. It was hard to believe that I was going home with Nan.

We got to the airport and checked in. When we got to the gate we found out that the flight would be delayed an hour. This meant that I had more time to wait in the airport. The instructor and I took Nan outside so she could take care of her needs, and then we came all the way back to the gate. We finally boarded the flight, and I was able to put Nan under the seat in front of me. She was that small. We flew down to Atlanta and had to go through that airport, which is very big. We would go through that airport many times in the months and years to come. When we first get the dogs the school does not want us working the dogs at that time because they are so new. I walked with the passenger assistant while I had Nan heel at my side. When I got my luggage we went out to the shuttle service to LaGrange. I got home in a little more than an hour after that. It felt good to be home. I got Nan acquainted with the apartment and relaxed. She had a lot to get used to. That night it felt good to sleep in my own bed. Nan slept well right next to me.

The next day I took it easy with Nan. We had to get used to each other. I had some chores to do around the house, and I had to wait for the cable company to rehook up my cable. Somehow they disconnected it thinking it was someone else's. I gave Nan the attention that she needed in a new situation.

On Sunday I took Nan out for a little walk in the area. She enjoyed the twenty minutes we were out and about. I had to get ready for the home instructor, who was going to be coming on Tuesday.

The next day I went to the office. I wanted to get Nan acquainted with the workplace. She did okay meeting all of the people at work. I found that she loved to have her belly rubbed. She started having me do that when I got her home. That evening I got out some of the toys that I had. She loved the tennis ball. She was so happy with it. I also had a squeaky toy and a rope that she also loved. That information was not in her puppy profile. She also loved to wag her tail. She would do it when she saw me. That was good.

On Tuesday the home instructor came and we talked about a strategy to work in LaGrange. We took a short walk through the square, and he started showing me various shops in the area. We would do more extensive work the next morning.

The next morning we started out by working the area around the square in LaGrange. There are a lot of shops in that area, and I learned how the square was laid out. I learned where the church was that I would be attending. To get there you had to walk down a big hill and cross a major street, which was about four lanes. It could be accomplished, however, with Nan's dedicated work. We had lunch in one of the restaurants in the area, which had great fried chicken. I really enjoyed that.

That afternoon we took Nan to the center where I was working and met the kids I would be working with in groups. One group in particular was made up of boys who were quite active. They were noisy and wanted to pet the dog. On numerous occasions the trainer had to remind the boys not to pet the dog unless they asked me. Nan really enjoyed the experience with all of the groups and wagged her tail and was happy to be with the kids.

The home trainer worked with me for another day or so. We went over different routes in town like going to the church and different stores in the square. We also went to the mall and worked there. Finally it was time for the instructor to depart and for me to go back to work. That was okay.

First Thanksgiving with Nan

It was Thanksgiving, and I had friends visit for the weekend. I cooked the traditional Thanksgiving dinner, and Nan was fine. Before the big day I ran errands in town, and Nan was a trouper. She really liked walking in the square. Later that weekend when my friends went home I went for a walk around the square. It took about forty-five minutes, and Nan and I really enjoyed the exercise. It was one of those crisp fall days that you get in November in that area.

First Christmas with Nan

I discovered that Nan did indeed like tennis balls. I had a bag of them in a closet in my house, and she found one and started playing with it. I also discovered that she liked a rope that I had with Murdock's toys that he never played with. She did, though, and enjoyed it very much. We would play tug of war all the time. I gave her other toys for Christmas.

When Christmas came closer I went to Virginia Beach to spend it with my mother and other relatives. We had a good time, and I received a lot of gifts. Nan and I took another plane trip, and she was great. I discovered that Nan is a good traveler, and that is wonderful.

In February my sister and my mom came to visit LaGrange. We went to the church that I learned the route to when the instructor was there. I wanted to see how Nan would behave in a church setting; she did great. I knew I could take her there, and that was terrific. It was almost like she was saying I can go anywhere with you. Even though they had seen her before they were impressed with how well behaved she was.

First communion

Another time when I attended that same church, on Palm Sunday to be exact, I went with a person whom I met in the church to receive communion. Nan led me up there, and when the priest tried to hand me the host he dropped it. It didn't even hit the floor. Nan caught it on the fly so to speak. So she received her first communion. Everyone got a kick out of that one. She just took it in stride and wagged her tail as if to say it's all in a day's work. I am proud of her for making such a great catch.

A good swimmer

I discovered that first summer that we were together that Nan is a great swimmer. I was at a friend's pool one Sunday afternoon. The pool area had a fence around it, so I let Nan loose in the area because she couldn't get out and she would be able to run a little and have some fun. I went in the pool, and a few minutes later I heard a big splash. What was that? I asked my neighbor; she told me that it was Nan jumping in the water. I was nervous, but she swam over to where I was as if to say look where I am. Swimming was natural to her, which is a characteristic of her breed. She really loved swimming. It takes about a year after you get your dog to find out what they are really like. You have to experience different events throughout the year to discover who they are. On another of our swims at that friend's pool I found out that Nan loves rubber barbells that squeak. When she swims she climbs out of the pool and runs around the area. She would run around with the barbell. The next Christmas she received one, which she loved.

A house full of puppies

I often wondered what Nan was like as a puppy. I got friendly with my neighbor downstairs, and on Thanksgiving I went with her to her daughter's for the day. They had Labrador puppies, so I got to see what they looked like. They were really cute and fuzzy. One wanted to chew my shoelaces. I held them and imagined what Nan looked like when she was that small. When the puppies would come into my lap Nan would bark at them as if to say "don't bother my dad."

She knew how to handle every situation she was in. One time we were visiting friends who had a boxer. He tried to attack Nan, but she just went into a corner and they had to get the dog and put him in another part of the house. That incident really scared me because I thought it would ruin her, but she was okay. I was glad for that.

Sometimes on my job I would visit kids in their home. Nan always let the kids rub her belly, and that made them feel more comfortable. Some kids were afraid of her, but others weren't. Basically, she loved what she was doing.

As I mentioned earlier, many times these dogs save our lives and we don't know it. One day I was starting to cross a street in LaGrange. Nan suddenly stopped and blocked my forward movement. A car had turned off the main street and crossed in front of me. If I didn't have her I really believe I would have been killed.

It is amazing how these dogs can take the initiative and rise to the occasion. My brother, sister-in-law, and two nephews came down to Georgia while they were visiting the eastern part of the country from California. The first day we went to Atlanta to see some of the sights there, and the next day we went to Huntsville, Alabama. What I am leading up to here is that when we were driving to Huntsville we stopped at a rest area to use the facilities and get something to drink. It was very warm and humid, and that drink would be very refreshing. When they got out of the car everyone went ahead of me into the rest area. It was raining, and I put Nan's harness on so she could lead me into the building. I had an idea where it was because we were on the interstate, so I was able to put the sound of the highway at my back. Nan took the initiative and found the door so I could go inside. That was great thinking on her part. She knew that I wanted to go in there. We spent the rest of that day visiting the space center that my brother wanted to see.

Ultimate patience

There were two times when Nan had to be very patient in a situation where she would have probably wanted to be somewhere else and she rose to the occasion nicely. That Christmas I went to Virginia Beach to visit my relatives. One cold day we went to the beach to be near the ocean for a few minutes. We were on the boardwalk where they strung

Christmas lights on the rail along the edge. Like I said earlier it was cold with no wind so you didn't feel it that much. It is neat how the ocean puts things into prospective. Anyway, we stood on the boardwalk with my niece and her husband who just came back from a deployment in the navy. Nan was lying there, and you could tell that she was cold. Her paws were under her body to keep her warm. She put up with it because she was with me.

After we finished with the boardwalk, we went to a nice restaurant for dinner. My niece's husband did not know that Nan was allowed in any restaurant by law. My niece had to enlighten him, which she did without any hesitation. We went to the restaurant, and Nan was very good. She just lay under the table, and when we got up to leave the people next to us commented that they did not know that a dog was there.

The other incident where Nan had to be very patient occurred on January 2, 2002, a couple of days after the boardwalk. We were flying back to Atlanta. When we landed it was snowing, which is a rare occurrence in that area. They were de-icing the planes, and flights were scattered all over the place. We sat on the runway for three hours waiting for a gate. I don't like being in planes that don't move, for some reason. I feel closed in. Nan somehow figured out that I was getting panicky and kept putting her paw on me as if to reassure me and say that it is okay. She had me rub her belly, which made me feel more relaxed in that situation.

We finally were able to go to a gate, and I was able to get off the plane and meet my friend who met me at the airport. We drove to LaGrange on snow-covered roads, which made the drive slow on the interstate. It sure felt good to get home that night. The next day Nan and I enjoyed the snow that was on the ground before it melted, which it did very quickly in that area. It was not like when I lived in Syracuse where the snow lasted forever.

A garden in the spring

I took Nan with me to Callaway Gardens in April of 2002 when I had a day off. My neighbor, sister, and mother went also. We had lunch in a restaurant that you had to get to by boat. That did not bother Nan in the least. After lunch we went to a building that had butterflies in it. It was set up like a tropical garden. Nan wanted to eat the butterflies when they settled on her nose. Luckily she didn't eat any. That was good. After we left the butterfly building we walked around the gardens.

A swim in the Gulf of Mexico

That fall over Columbus Day weekend Nan and I went with my neighbor and her daughter to Destin, Florida, which is on the Gulf Coast, in the Panhandle to be specific. They were going down there to go deep-sea fishing. I was going to stay with her daughter and her granddaughter while the other members of the family went fishing. The evening we got there we had dinner in a restaurant where we sat on a porch right over the beach and I could hear the waves. That was great.

The next morning while the others were out fishing I took Nan to the beach where she could swim in the gulf. She really enjoyed that. She wanted to drink the water and could not understand that it was salty. The hotel I was staying in gave me old towels to dry her with when I got back to the room. When the others got back from fishing we went out for dinner at another seafood restaurant.

The next morning we went to a pancake house for breakfast, which was better than what the hotel served. They served one of those continental breakfasts, which were not good at all in my opinion. We had a better breakfast at the pancake house. Nan was good for the most part at the restaurant. While we were going to our table the waitress dropped someone's stack of pancakes, and Nan took it upon herself to take some of them. She really enjoyed that surprise snack, which landed right under her nose as she was walking to our table. We all had a good time there.

A move to Virginia

In January of 2003 I left the job in LaGrange for numerous reasons and decided to move to Virginia to be closer to family. I also wanted to get a job in a school setting. I had been planning this move for a couple of months, and in January I decided to do it. That Christmas I traveled to Long Island to visit relatives, and after consulting with them I made my decision. My mother and I were planning to purchase and move into a condo in Virginia Beach. That would happen in early May when the condo was available. Nan and I had to learn a new area, which would be fun. At the end of February, Nan and I made the move.

When we took the plane from Atlanta I put Nan under the seat in front of me like extra baggage. She was very quiet, and when we arrived in Norfolk the people around me remarked that they did not know a dog was on the plane. I told them that she was always that good. So I was now in Virginia and would see how things would go.

My mom lived in a large apartment complex that was tricky to get around. Everything looked the same, and you could get confused easily. When we moved to the condo it would be in an area where there were streets and sidewalks. There also was a pool in the community that I could learn to get to in the summer.

So we moved into the condo in May, and someone from the Seeing Eye came by and showed me the neighborhood. Nan caught on quickly, and we had it mastered in a couple of days. I believe that the older these dogs get the smarter they become.

For the rest of the spring I adjusted to the new neighborhood, which was quite easy to get around once I got the hang of it.

One time I was in the grocery store and I had Nan with me. While I was walking around in the store Nan suddenly started wagging her tail. I wondered what that was about. Then I heard a youngster's voice, who I guessed was about twelve. I could tell that he was mentally challenged. He started petting Nan; his mom told him to ask me first. He did, and I let him. He really enjoyed that. Nan somehow knew that he was the way he was, and that is amazing. It was like she had a sixth sense.

A trip to Long Island and Florida

That summer I took two trips, one to Long Island and the other to Daytona Beach, Florida. Earlier that summer a friend who was in my class when I was getting Nan came up from Florida. We went to the pool that I mentioned earlier and to different restaurants in the area. We did a lot of walking with the dogs and got a lot of exercise. That was good for both of us.

A couple of days after my birthday I took that trip to Long Island to attend my great nephew's christening. They had the ceremony at the church and then a party at a fancy restaurant. While we were there we stayed in a motel, and Nan learned where to go in the hotel for various things like the breakfast bar. The rooms had Braille numbers on them, so I knew how to get back to my room when I wanted to go there. Nan was very confident in that motel. We drove up and back; she was very good in the van. We also went to a couple of restaurants and visited relatives who lived in the area.

On our way back to Virginia we decided to take a ferry across Delaware Bay. It was very rough, and the boat was really rolling in the swells. I almost got seasick, but Nan handled it like a trouper. While we were on the boat we met a girl who raised puppies for the Seeing Eye. She told me what it was like and that Nan looked like the puppy she raised. I told her that Nan had been out in the field for a couple of years. I was sure glad to be done with that ferry ride. I vowed never to do that again without making sure that the weather was good. The rest of the trip home went off without a hitch.

The next week I went to Florida to visit the friend who came up to visit me the previous month. The flight went well. I had to change in

Atlanta, but I got to my connecting gate okay. When I got to Florida I went to my friend's house and relaxed for the rest of the day.

The next day we went to a mall and had a buffet lunch. We had to dodge tropical showers during the day. We also went to an agency that serves blind people in the area so my friend could visit with some of the people attending the center. We did a lot of walking, and Nan got a good workout.

The next day we hung around the house and that evening went to a happy hour at a local bar. We had to walk home from the bar, and Nan remembered where the house was. That was great.

The next day we went to a restaurant on the beach and had a seafood meal. My friend also had her dog with her, and they behaved very well. I met a child in the restaurant who was about five years old, and Nan let him rub her belly. They both enjoyed themselves. She loved meeting kids.

While I was there we took talking buses; they had a system on the bus that told you where it was via GPS. I found that to be very interesting. We went to other malls and walked around Daytona Beach, where my friend lived. One day we must have walked a couple of miles. I probably lost some weight on that trip.

A bad hurricane

It is amazing how these dogs tune in to different situations. In September of 2003 we had a bad hurricane in the Hampton Roads area. I was concerned about taking Nan outside with possible trees coming down in the wind. Well, we went outside, and she did what she had to do and then dragged me back into the house where it was safe. She knew that something was going on. It is amazing in these storms how you have a lull once in a while, so I would listen for one and when it happened I would take her outside so she could take care of her needs. That was a long day in the house hunkering down and listening to the wind and rain. We were glad when it was over.

A trip to my grade school

In October of 2003 I went to a reunion in the grade school I attended, which was located in the Bronx, New York. It was a school for blind children. I remembered the layout of the building, so I was able to show Nan around. She handled it very well. I told her that "this was where Daddy went to school." She wagged her tail when I told her that. It was amazing what I remembered about that building. It sure brought back memories for me. I saw my eighth-grade classroom, where we heard about the Kennedy assassination in 1963. I was glad I was able to share those memories with Nan. The next year they were going to have the hundredth anniversary of the school. More about that later. While I was there I stayed on Long Island and had a good time. We went to a nice restaurant and had German food for Oktoberfest. Nan and I really enjoyed that. In New York they have a lot of bake shops where you can get fresh baked cookies and things. We visited one while I was there. Someone dropped a couple of cookies on the floor, and Nan helped herself to them without hesitation. They also gave her doggy cookies that they made for dogs that came into the shop, which she enjoyed a lot.

Seventy-fifth anniversary

In June of 2004 I attended the seventy-fifth anniversary of the Seeing Eye in Morristown. There must have been three or four hundred dog teams at a picnic that they had for the graduates commemorating this milestone in their history. The dogs were really well behaved, and Nan got her belly rubbed by her trainer. She enjoyed that. The people who were in attendance came from all over the United States. The picnic was very elegant, as only the Seeing Eye can do it. Everyone really enjoyed themselves. I was glad I could attend.

To get there I had to take a plane from Norfolk, Virginia, where I lived, a couple of days later a train on the Long Island Railroad, and the Jersey Transit train to Morristown. Nan did the trip like the trouper that she is. She had no problem negotiating Penn Station. That place is a challenge for anyone.

Later that week I went back into the city to meet someone for lunch. We went to Outback Steakhouse, which was very nice. Nan negotiated the city streets without any trouble. We took the subway, which must have brought back memories of the training days when she was brought into New York. She was very businesslike, because I had to go through Penn Station during rush hour. It was wall-to-wall people, but we got through it okay and took the Long Island Railroad back to Hicksville. We were both exhausted after that trip. I was glad I went to meet my friend for lunch.

Nan has a boyfriend

In the fall of 2004 I had to go to Arkansas to take a course for possible work. There was a woman attending the school with me who had a Seeing Eye dog named Jagger. Nan and he became best friends. They would play with each other in the lounge at the school. Jagger would look out for Nan. It was real cute. They had two relief areas for the dogs, one with grass and the other with cement. Nan preferred to use the grass unless it was raining. If Jagger was out there when Nan was there he would wait until Nan was finished and came by to go in so he would know that she was okay. It was so cute seeing that. They really were fond of each other.

I would go to Long Island and stay with a friend who had a male dog who also looked out for Nan, especially when we went anywhere. In fact, he would whimper when Nan and I would go home. He missed Nan being around. It is cute that Nan has that effect on the male dogs that she knows.

Hundredth anniversary

In October of 2004 I attended the hundredth anniversary of the Lavelle School for the Blind, which I attended for elementary school. They had a luncheon for us, which was one of the most elegant affairs that I ever attended. They had a cocktail hour and the lunch afterward, and the food was out of this world. It was held at the New York Botanical Garden, which was a beautiful setting for such a luncheon. I saw my eighth-grade teacher who at eighty-nine was still in good health, which I was glad to see. She remembered me, which surprised me. As I said before, the food was out of this world.

Nan handled the experience very well. It involved a lot of flying on planes and negotiating the facility where the party took place. There were other guide dogs, and they were all very good. Nan made a lot of new friends at that party. I enjoyed seeing people whom I hadn't seen in forty years. It is amazing how the staff members remembered me after all of that time. After the weekend I flew back to Arkansas to continue the course I was taking down there.

A trip to Las Vegas

In the summer of 2005 Nan and I went to Las Vegas for a convention. It was so hot out there I had to get her special boots so she would not burn her feet on the hot pavement. I didn't know how she would like wearing those boots, so I had her wear them before I left. I was able to get a pair for her, which was great. I had her wear the boots around the house and when I took her out.

I also had a five-hour flight to be concerned about. Would she be able to handle that long a time on a plane? I had never had her on a plane for that long of a stretch. Well, she came through with flying colors. I am glad I had those boots, because you could literally fry an egg on the sidewalks out there. It got up to 108; very hot. They say that you don't feel the heat when it is dry, but I don't believe that.

At least the hotel was air conditioned, and we had a good time at the conference. There were a lot of nice restaurants in the hotel, and in the morning I was able to go out to breakfast when it was cooler and get Nan some exercise. In that area it cools down overnight even though the day is very hot.

Of course I played the slot machines and I won five hundred dollars one time. I was thrilled about that. We had a good week, and Nan worked very well. She got along with the other dogs at the convention.

Substitute teaching

In October of 2005 I signed up for substitute teaching in my local schools in Virginia Beach. The process was quite involved. It consisted of my filing applications and having a physical. I even had to be fingerprinted. I was going to teach kindergarten through eighth grade. Nan would be going with me to the schools, so I knew that she would be a big hit with the kids for the most part. I waited for about five months until I got an assignment. I had to attend a couple of seminars to prepare myself for subbing.

My first assignment was in a middle school, which worked out very well. I did various things, and one of the teachers in that school was a personal friend of mine. Nan took the experience in stride. She guided me through the halls with all of the kids moving everywhere, and the experience did not bother her at all. In fact, she enjoyed the challenge of it.

The real challenge was when I was in the cafeteria where the kids would drop French fries and other food on the floor. I had to keep on top of her, but she helped herself to a couple of French fries and things anyway. She could not help herself.

We were a great hit with the kids. They were amazed at how well we worked together. I also brought electronic equipment with me that helped me with reading and other things, and the kids really loved that. My first day went very well.

Another day that spring I worked with second graders, and that was really a lot of fun. They all petted Nan when I took her harness off, and she let them rub her belly. They thought it was the coolest thing having a dog in the class. At times I had to put Nan under my desk so the kids could get their work done. I would show a video from the Seeing Eye when I would work in these classes, which showed them how they train a dog like Nan. The kids would always love it when they would show the puppies on the video.

Having Nan and me in the class was a good learning experience for them. It pointed out to them that a person with a disability could make something of themselves. I really enjoyed subbing.

Another day I worked in a fourth-grade class, and those kids were really nice. They all cooperated with us, and when it was time to go home they all came over and petted Nan and gave me a hug. That was a great day.

Another day I worked in a fifth-grade class where the students acted out a lot. I was told later that the day Nan and I were in there the kids were on their best behavior. One of the kids lived in my condo and was so excited to see me. In fact, he comes by to visit me once in a while. I saw another kid from that class up at the pool in my neighborhood that summer. He was glad to see us.

One other day I worked in a class in a middle school where the kids had severe emotional problems. The class was in one of the portable buildings that the school had. I was told that one student in particular was very troublesome and I might have difficulty with him. As it turned out Nan and I were a great influence on him. He was very cooperative with me and Nan and was very helpful to us. He had his best day when we were there. Nan really looked out for him.

Nan could really adapt to each situation. One day that fall I worked in a class where the students were mentally challenged. They really enjoyed having me in that class. Nan and I received a lot of hugs that day. We helped the kids go to different activities around the building like gym. The kids really looked out for us and made sure I knew what to do. When I went back to that class I always got a big welcome.

Another experience shows you how adaptable Nan is: One day I worked with a girl who was in a wheelchair in a middle school. Nan and I would help her get around the building, and I would get things out of her locker for her as she needed them. I would also help her with her computer and other materials that she needed to do her work in class. Nan would patiently wait until we would have to go somewhere with her.

The last subbing story I will share with you is about when I worked in a kindergarten class. The kids really got a kick out of having Nan and me in there. They all enjoyed playing with her, and she was so good with kids that small. I helped them open their milks and their syrup packets so they could eat their lunch. They were having pancakes, so I had to help them with that. Nan just lay patiently under the table, and I had to stop the kids from feeding her many times. Later I saw one of the kids in Wal-Mart and he remembered me.

A good sport

On March 23, 2007, I attended the retirement of a friend of mine from the navy. He was serving on the Bainbridge which was a destroyer. The retirement ceremony was held on the deck of the ship, outdoors, and the weather was beautiful. Nan went out on to the peer and found the ramp to board the ship. We had to go through narrow passageways and doors with airlocks where you had to close one door before you opened the other in front of you. The stairs were very steep: in fact they were ladders. We had to get Nan up and down these staircases. We literally had to carry her up and down. She took the whole experience in stride.

The ceremony was very nice. The crew paid a nice tribute to my retiring friend. When we came on board they announced that my friend was on the ship. They presented him and his family with awards and the retirement plaque.

After the ceremony we went down to the chief's mess to have cake and punch or coffee if you wanted it. Nan worked like the trouper she is. The staff members on the ship were very courteous to all of us. They were impressed at how Nan handled guiding me through the vessel. When it was time to get off she guided me through those narrow passageways and up the ladder where we had to carry her up the stairs because they were too steep for her to negotiate. That experience really showed me how patient and willing Nan is to endure anything to be with me.

Consequently, the party that we went to at my friend's house was a lot easier for her to handle. In fact, it was a lot of fun with good food. All in all it was a beautiful day.

A trip to the Amish Country

About a month after the retirement ceremony on the ship Nan and I went to the Amish Country in Pennsylvania. We went with a church group on a bus trip. The bus was nice and Nan was okay about it. The only thing was that the hydraulic system made a high-pitched noise, which made her a little nervous. I didn't make a big deal out of it because if I did it would only reinforce the nervous behavior. I had to point out to her that things were okay.

We went to an Amish restaurant and had a feast. Nan almost got a bowl of mashed potatoes when someone almost dropped the bowl. She would have enjoyed that one. The food was excellent. It was family style; we passed around the different things they served us. Even the dessert was great.

That night we went to a theater, and the music in the performance was wonderful. Nan found the music to be very relaxing.

The next morning we went to the Amish market and a dairy farm. They had the cows in a large barn. The bus was able to drive right into the building, and we could see the cows being milked. Nan was sure curious about those animals. She sat up with her nose up against the bus window looking at those cows. Knowing her, she wanted to go out and make friends with them. I am sure she wondered what was going on out there.

We had more great food at another restaurant, and then we headed home. That was a great trip.

A big challenge

About a week or two later I went to Long Island for some family business. I got a chance to go into Manhattan to visit a friend for lunch. It meant going on the Long Island Railroad, taking the subway from Pennsylvania Station, and taking a cross-town bus to the east side of Manhattan. That was quite a challenge for Nan, but she did great. When we were crossing one of the streets a cab pulled out in front of us and Nan had to stop short to keep me from getting hit. A lot of people really swore at that cab driver, and the folks on the street commended Nan for doing such good work.

My friend and I had a nice lunch together at a good restaurant. We walked around the neighborhood, and Nan and I got a lot of exercise.

When we were going back to Penn Station I got off the subway and was not sure where I was. I tried to ask for directions, but a lot of people had headphones on and could not hear me. As it turned out we were going in the right direction. Nan remembered how to get me back into the station so I could catch the train back to Long Island. It goes to show you that if you trust the dog you will get to where you need to go safely.

Conclusion

Well, this brings us to the end of this journey. Forty years is a long time to have memories of five Seeing Eye dogs. I must say that I would not trade these memories for anything in the world. I know that I can go anywhere with the knowledge that I will be safe and secure with Nan. In fact, that was the case with all of the dogs that I have had.

If you trust the dog they will get you where you need to go safely. I have to know where I am going and be aware of my surroundings. If I need directions I can ask people on the street just as anyone else does. Nan will guide me with confidence and grace.

I hope that reading this book heightened your awareness of how precious and dedicated these dogs really are. Even after all of this time, every day is an adventure. Nan is ten now, and I hope we will be together another couple of years. She is really a fun dog, one who does her work well but loves to play with her toys and have her belly rubbed. That is small pay for what they do for us. All they ask is that we praise them for doing good work. That isn't much to ask. These dogs are really our true friends.

Breinigsville, PA USA
19 November 2009
227859BV00002B/2/P